Give Yourself Credit
Money Doesn't Grow On Trees!

Copyright © 2010
by David E. Robinson

Fifth Edition, September, 2011

This information is offered for educational purposes only; not to be taken as legal advice. These statements might be true — or false.

All Rights Reserved
Parts of this book may be reproduced subject to due and specific acknowledgment of their source.

MAINE-PATRIOT.com
3 Linnell Circle
Brunswick, Maine 04011

maine-patriot.com

GIVE YOURSELF CREDIT

GOD BLESS AMERICA

Money Doesn't Grow On Trees

Give Yourself Credit

Contents

Acceptance For Value ---------------- 13
1 National, Debt-Free Money ------------------------ 15
2 Dismal Deflation ----------------------------------- 19
3 Good Times & Bad --------------------------------- 21
4 Real Wealth Production -------------------------- 27
5 Shelter, Clothing & Food ------------------------- 31
6 Implications of HJR 192 of 1933 ----------------- 37
7 Money Without Debt ------------------------------ 47
8 The Money Issue ---------------------------------- 53
9 Follow Through ------------------------------------ 59
10 Orchestrated Results ----------------------------- 61
11 Conditions Now ------------------------------------ 63
12 How Banks Operate ------------------------------- 67
13 Balance Your Account ---------------------------- 73
14 Overcoming Debt With Knowledge -------------- 77
15 Commercial Redemption ------------------------- 81
16 The Mark, The Name, Or The Number ---------- 83
17 Equity-Interest Recovery ------------------------ 85

18	Watch What You Say	95
19	You Have A Bond	99
20	Your Supersedeas Bond	101
21	Your Mirror-Image Strawman	105
22	Promissory Notes Are Legal Tender	115
23	We The People Provide The Credit	117
24	The Truth Now Told	119
25	Remedy Review	125
26	It's Only A Game	129
27	Recall Notice	133

Handling Presentments

Acceptance for Value — *via the IRS* ---------- 143

Appendix

28	The Business of Business	165
29	As It Is Today	173
30	After Moving In for $16 He's Ready	181
31	Lawful Basis of Acceptance for Value --	185

HJR 192 of June 5, 1933 -------------- 195

Final Word ---------------------- 201

LAND OF THE FREE

Money Doesn't Grow On Trees

"Behold, I stand at the door, and knock: if any man hear my voice, and open the door, I will come in to him, and will sup with him, and he with me." — *Jesus the Christ at Revelation 3:20.*

Rockwell "Family Grace" 1938

GIVE US THIS DAY OUR DAILY BREAD

MY GOD SHALL SUPPLY ALL YOUR NEED ACCORDING TO HIS RICHES IN GLORY BY CHRIST JESUS

GIVE YOURSELF CREDIT

Acceptance For Value

When you receive a bill from a corporation it is not really a bill, it is a check that you can turn into a money order per HJR 192 of June 5, 1933.

Since 1933, no one in America has been able to lawfully "pay" a debt. Payment of debt is now against congressional Public Policy. Henceforth every debt obligation shall be "discharged."

The United States went bankrupt in 1933, by filing Chapter 11, so there is no more gold or silver to back our money supply. We are Creditors of the United States, so we can turn any debt instrument into a credit instrument with which we can pay our debts, with our signature.

FRNs (Federal Reserve Notes) are debt instruments and you cannot "pay" a debt with more debt. Minus $10 dollars, *minus* minus $10 dollars = minus $20 dollars.

We create money with our signature.

We generate the funds that create the money at the Federal Reserve by the energy of our labor. We can discharge all debt with our "credit-sign" (our signature) backed by the future commercial energy that we will produce.

When you get a "presentment" (a traffic ticket, a bill, or a summons, etc.) you can discharge the presented charge.

The bill (the presentment) is a check. "Accept for Value" the presentment, and turn it into a money order — endorse it on the back as you would to deposit a check, and return it to the presenter or send it to the IRS.

GIVE YOURSELF CREDIT

1
National, Debt-Free Money

There is no reason for us to put up with recession, depression, and unemployment.

By using 2006 statistics, we can see that the U.S. Gross Domestic Product (GDP) came to about $14 trillion dollars, while the total income of the nation came to only about $10 trillion dollars, and at least 10% of that income was reinvested income rather than income spent on goods and services.

The total available purchasing power of the nation was only about $10 trillion dollars, or about $4 trillion dollars less than the total collective price of goods and services.

Where did consumers get the extra $4 trillion dollars? They had to borrow it from the banks that created it out of nothing with simple accounting entries on their books.

If the government were to replace this bank-created-out-of-nothing money with **national, debt-free money,** instead, the total money supply would remain unchanged and a whopping $4 trillion dollars in new *government issued* **national, debt-free money** would be fed into the economy without increasing the inflation rate, and this *government issued* **national, debt-free money** could be used to pay a guaranteed basic income for all Americans — such as $10,000 per adult and $5,000 per each dependent child — each year, — *instead of paying needless interest to the private, non-federal, Federal Reserve banks.*

Money Doesn't Grow On Trees

If $4 trillion dollars of newly created, **national, debt-free money** were issued to fill the gap between GDP and our purchasing power, and this $4 trillion dollars of new, **national, debt-free money** were distributed among the people, the government would still have over $1 trillion dollars each year to satisfy its budgetary needs without a federal income tax.

By utilizing **national, debt-free money** Congress could stabilize prices, and output would increase to full employment.

There is no reason for us to put up with recession, depression and unemployment. The government simply has to put more money into circulation.

It can all be paid for if the government increased the money supply by issuing **national, debt-free money,** as Lincoln did at the start of the Civil War.

We suffer from a failure of consumer demand because of a lack of buying power — because of our failure to use our God-given **national credit** to prime the pump.

Our country was pulled out of the Depression by priming the pump with liquidity and funding new projects that put new money into the people's pocket.

Watering a liquidity starved economy with new, **national, debt-free money,** — instead of borrowing money at interest from the banks *and then giving it back to the banks* — would work wonders.

People want to work and there is work to be done.

Consumers want to purchase the fruits of their labor but they can't because of the anemic money supply. An infusion of new, **national, debt-free money** — instead of borrowing more interest laden debt from the banks — would get the wheels of production turning again.

Very little of borrowed money goes to improve infrastructure or to increase employment. Jobs are being out-sourced abroad while the public struggles to make the interest payments on the *needless federal debt* . . . and stay alive.

2
Dismal Deflation

Deflation is a shortage of the people's buying power relative to the power of the nation to produce. But when production is cut-down, as usually happens in a depression, then workers lose their jobs and the people's buying power is still further reduced relative to the power of the nation to produce.

The country and the people get progressively poorer, and nobody profits except the people who either have hoarded money, or the people who have the power to create it in the first place, such as the banks. For all they have to do is sit on their money or their power to create it and watch the price of everything go down to their advantage, which means that the purchasing power of their withheld money goes up correspondingly.

"Depression" is another word for "deflation." Depressions are never caused by "over-production." They are caused by under consumption which is, in turn, caused by a lack of buying power in the hands of would be consumers.

So the one and only thing to do when faced with deflation is to increase the buying power of the people.

The first thing that is needed is the creation of an *additional* supply of new money in such a way as to not increase debt — so that it will be available to the masses of the people for expenditures on the services and goods which producers are eager and needing to produce and sell.

To put the matter simply and concisely, the general thing that is needed when deflation threatens — as like now — is to have Congress or its appointed agency create the proper amount of **national, debt-free money** or **debt-free credit** on the Treasury books and use it to expand the present monetary system into a national program that will put active buying power directly into the hands of our people who will spend it for the general good.

There is simply no good reason why the people of this nation should be called upon to suffer through another period of deflation and business stagnation. Not if Congress does its constitutional duty as we insist.

There is no need to fear inflation as long as our national productive capacity is not exceeding its 100 percent capacity to produce.

3
Good times & Bad

That which happened to America after the Stock Market crash of 1929 was something like what happened to America in 1896 when for the first time disappointed and penniless seekers after homestead land started to trek back Eastward again, having found that the last good prairie land was gone and that the lands they had tried to farm could not sustain their families, under those circumstances.

For two and a half centuries Americans had taken completely for granted that they could move West and make a new start whenever they needed to.

These dejected land seekers coming back East symbolized the end of an epoch full of hope for the common folks.

So at the close of 1929 and in 1930 America faced for the first time the fact that her old methods of achieving economic and industrial expansion could not continue forever any more than her people's search for fertile farmlands in the West. Another great American epoch had come to an end.

So when the "New Deal" was born under Franklin Delano Roosevelt, we reacted in accordance with the law of self-preservation because we instinctively knew that times like those of the past were gone and were never coming back because of the increasing division of labor, the increasing inter-dependence of the people, and the complete absence of a free land frontier.

The tremendous obstacles to people of little means in surviving the Great Depression and starting over again meant that the country could not again stand a period when the government just stood by and watched the credit structure collapse.

Periods of bankruptcy were the price that had to be paid for the government letting the economic life of the country alone, no matter come what may. For under the debt-laden money system that we have today, periods of "boom" brought about by the credit expansion of private banks must always be followed by periods of unemployment and depression.

When credit contraction takes place and unsupportable debt burdens are allowed to collapse and be written off in bankruptcy, economic hopelessness and loss affect millions of people and many businesses too.

The ancient Hebrews had a better way. Every seven years they cancelled all debt and started over freshly anew. The farmers didn't have to give up their farms and families didn't have to give up their homes. So their system worked very well.

Only by using the most illogical and utterly unsound measures can industrial expansion be supported today under the debt monetary and financial system we use.

Some of those illogical and unsound methods of attempting to make the economic system of today "add up" have already been tried.

Only at times, when a net addition to the purchasing power of the people over and above that paid out by industry, has there been full employment and prosperity in recent times. For industry never distributes enough buying power to enable the people to buy the increasing amount of goods that it can and does turn out.

So it is almost always true that modern industries can increase their output of goods without any corresponding increase in the amount of money they pay out in wages, interest, rent, or dividends, into the hands of consumers.

So something else has to happen to make up this deficiency of consumer buying power, or the goods produced can't be sold. A War for example is one of the illogical and certainly tragic and wasteful ways the economic system can be gotten to "add up."

During a war the government borrows a lot of money from the banks, at interest, and spends in on armaments and troops. Armaments are something the people can't buy, though they receive wages for producing it. And all other industries gain this additional buying power to add to what they pay out themselves. It keeps them going by giving them a dependable market for which to produce.

Of course the cost of war requires a tremendous addition to the National Debt.

But War wasn't the only thing that kept our industries going in pre- "New Deal" times.

During the 1920's, America *gave away,* up 'till the Depression, *about $22 billion dollars worth of goods!* That is, we produced them and shipped them abroad and never got paid for them. We gave foreigners buying power over American goods. This was one way of "developing a market." Part of it was the result of the sales in the United States of worthless foreign bonds during the 1920's.

Also, state and local governments increased their indebtedness by $10 trillions dollars and spent it into the hands of

Money Doesn't Grow On Trees

the people who in turn spent it into the economy for services and goods. And consumer's during the 1920's went into debt buying goods on the installment plan, to the amount of another $10 trillion dollars by 1929. Americans took off of the market that much more goods than they had money in hand to pay for at the time.

These were some of the stop-gaps that made it *appear* that all was well and gave a false sense of security to the American people until the crash of 1929. But the crash did come. That depression seemed more like an abyss than a depression.

For example: We became afraid that machines were going to take more and more jobs away from the people. With monopolies at work and a debt money system that only produced buying power by increasing debt, machine production was always out-running the buying power of consumers.

Machines *might not* create unemployment if so many of the machines were not controlled by monopolistic combinations and concerns. Monopolies and machines, and technological improvements, *do* cause unemployment because monopolies maintain high prices and restrict output. Monopolies siphon off the benefits of the machines into huge corporate surpluses made possible by very excess profits.

Under true competition, the benefits of the machines would go to consumers in lower prices and to the producers too, because consumers would have greater purchasing power than before.

The Anti-Trust Division of the Justice Department and the Tennessee Valley Authority had the effect of breaking down monopoly price structures and reducing the cost of goods and services to consumers.

Between 1922 and 1929 the output per worker in the United States increased by 18 percent. So one of three things had to happen. Either the price of goods had to decline 18 percent, so the people would be able to buy 18 percent more goods with the available supply of money; or there had to be 18 percent more money created and put into the hands of the people, who could spend it and buy 18 percent more goods at the old prices; or else 18 percent of the workers would have to be let go; fired.

Unless one of the first two things were done, it would be necessary to fire workers, because industry could produce as much as it had done before with 18 percent fewer people.

Monopoly *control of industry* prevents a reduction of *prices,* and monopoly *control of finance* prevents an increase in the *volume of money.* So the third thing happens and a lot of people lose their jobs.

A general reduction of prices has never happened before in a free economy. Never has there been a period of prosperity when the price level was going down. Furthermore, over a long period of time, wages do constantly continue to rise.

In other words, the answer to machines and increased efficiency is increased *buying power* for the common man. The central question is, then, shall the additional money needed to supply this necessary increase in buying power be provided by the government creating the additional money needed interest free? Or must oppressive debt always intervene and bring collapse and depression in its wake?

If the buying power of the dollar is effectively kept at a constant level, and if the people as a whole through their Congress exercise their power to create money, interest free when economic circumstances demand it, then monopolies and the *destitutions upon true economic liberty* will be removed. For no power on earth makes monopoly control of real wealth *so easy to achieve* as the power of private banks to create and expand money at interest.

Had the big city banks not been able to create their money by ink marks on paper out of thin air, it would have been much more difficult for competing firms to be bought out, or for control over these industries to be taken over by financial concerns. And nothing has contributed as much to the destruction of small scale business as changes in the purchasing power of the dollar. It has always been at such times that farmers have lost their farms and banks and insurance companies have become landlords, and little businesses have gone under, leaving their financially powerful competitors to control an even greater share of the market when the cycle turned upward again.

By 1929 one-third of our people could produce all of the necessities of life needed by all the people. And unless all the people were able to consume their share of the necessities, even that one-third couldn't keep their jobs.

What those businessmen needed was more demand for the goods that they had capacity to produce and sell. The only answer to consumer demand in peace time is a higher standard of living for the people generally; whereas under the present debt-money system the only way buying power can be increased is by expansion of someone's debt.

Nearly all our money is created by the banks writing up demand deposits out of thin air and using them to make interest bearing loans. But debt expansion cannot go on forever. Sooner or later, debt has to be paid.

4
Real Wealth Production

The limiting factor in the production of real wealth has been the failure to distribute to would-be consumers enough money to buy the *potential output* of the producers of services and goods.

If the distribution throughout the nation of the purchasing power necessary to enable the nation to consume the whole of their total production, were enough, they could equally consume the goods of other nations as well which they might exchange for their production.

Any nation can safely credit itself with new-money-income and pay it into active circulation up to a certain easily determined total amount. That amount is the number of new dollars that can be put into circulation without prices increasing. The danger of inflation comes only when too much money is being put into circulation relative to the supply of goods. Therefore inflation and deflation menace a nation only when the nation has inadequate control over the creation and retirement of its circulating media of exchange.

Paying off portions of the National Debt can counter inflation any time it threatens if those payments are properly employed.

And deflation — the worst menace to the common people of limited means — could be prevented according to a mandate of a caring Congress, if a governmental authority exclusively responsible for the creation of new money and national credit promptly placed in circulation enough new purchasing power to check any decline in the price of goods.

We will not have inflation or deflation if these things are done.

But with the private banks having the power to destroy or create money at will, through their technique of fractional reserve banking, inflation and deflation will alternately plague the people, off and on, as it is doing and has done in the past.

The thing that leads to dangerous inflation is not the creation of money by government, but a continuous increase in public debt. For whenever an interest-bearing debt becomes so large that its servicing requires a major portion of tax revenue so large that the people lose hope of ever being able to pay it off, then comes the temptation to reduce or eliminate the debt by unsound, unjust, artificial means — such as repudiation or by needless War.

And it is then when inflation may come in in earnest, not as an accident or a consequence of other factors, but as a deliberate policy of a distressed people.

While needless war is going on there are other costs that concern the people far more than the financial ones or the soaring National Debt: namely, the loss of lives most of all.

The most important thing about war-finance, and tomorrows money, is that other methods become known and put into effect whereby the people can escape the ever-mounting interest charges of the banks by earning their way out from under the debt that war leaves behind in its wake.

Under a scientific, interest-free, monetary system any people can and will earn their way out of debt if they increase their national production of real services and goods.

And so we come to the final and truly hopeful point. A scientific, interest-free monetary system requires the rate of the increase of money in circulation to be the same as the rate of the increase of the production of goods.

And this increase of revenue must not come from taxes or from borrowing; nor by adding one thin dime to the National Debt. This increase of revenue must consist of new, interest-free money created without cost to anyone, by the issuing authority of the People's Congress where its validity and buying power have already been secured by the prior production of the things for which this revenue has already been used to buy — hence the established principle of *mutual offset credit exemption exchange.*

The American people can earn their way out of the National Debt under the sort of scientific interest-free monetary system described in this book.

5
Shelter, Clothing & Food

The war that broke out upon the world, in September, 1939, was not just the Second World War. Not only was it a clash between one group of nations and another group, it was a world-wide struggle between two fundamentally different systems of government and philosophies of human life. The real victory is yet to be won or lost, not only by military might, but by enlisting the profound allegiance of the peoples of the world to one system or the other — the fight to the death between the slave world and the free.

The "four freedoms" enunciated by President Franklin Delano Roosevelt in his message to Congress, on January 6, 1941, are the very core of the revolution for which the United Nations have taken their stand.

We who live in the United States might think that there is nothing revolutionary about **Freedom of religion, Freedom of expression,** and **Freedom from the fear of secret police,** but when we think about the significance of **Freedom from want for the common man,** we see that the revolution of the past 200 years has not as yet been won, either here in the United States or in any other nation of the world. And we know that this revolution cannot stop until **Freedom from** want has eventually actually been attained. Those who *write the peace* must think of the whole world. We ourselves here in the United States are no more a master race than were the Nazis of Roosevelt's time.

Waging war *with our neighbors in the world* cannot but be a part of a profound transformation of the lives of all men and women around the world — for good or ill.

The forces of revolution and change derive their power from the bafflement and confusion of the age.

Why should men be unemployed when they themselves need the things they can and want to produce?

Why should people go hungry while farmers lose their land because they cannot sell their crops for a living price?

Why, indeed, should there be a depression and unemployment when producers want to work and when consumers are in dire need of the things the producers want to and could make available and sell today?

Why should "deflation" and "scarcity of money" stand in the way of fulfilling these fundamental human needs?

These old and threadbare questions lie at the root of the unrest that is rocking and shaking the world.

Ever since the beginning there have been these things that men have sought after. The first has been *food, warmth, and shelter:* the basic necessities of life. The second has been *security, or safety, and freedom from fear.* And the third has been *liberty of spirit: the right to call one's soul one's own.* And as man has progressed from age to age men have tended to value more and more the third of these things: *liberty of spirit.*

But with the coming of the industrial revolution the direct connection between man's labor and the supplying of his physical needs was broken. The division of labor into specialized tasks has practically destroyed the relationship that once existed between daily work and the production of man's own shelter, clothing, and food. Thus *unemployment appeared.*

Not for long can people tolerate a situation where they are told that they cannot work because there is no "demand" for their labor when at the same time they find their families in want. For they will say: "But there is a demand for us to work; there is a demand that we produce *shelter, clothing, and food.* For our families demand and need these things."

And while all this is true, they will be told, nevertheless, that "enough has already been produced." To which the people reply: "Then why can't we satisfy our families needs?"

But the wise ones will say, "But you have no money."

And to that the reply, should be: "Then give us the money and we will consume the surplus goods, and then there will be jobs for us and work for us to do."

And to this the answer comes: "But that would make you objects of government charity. It is better for you to remain unemployed."

Not for long will men endure the utter foolishness of such answers to their questions. So dictators arise who tell the people that they will trade them jobs for the right to rule over them for all time. Thereby men have been forced by needless circumstances to give up the third great and most valuable objective of their search — *liberty of spirit* — in order, as they have been led to believe, that they might gain the first — *food, and the other necessities of life for their families and themselves* — purchased at the price of freedom and liberty.

So we become determined, therefore, to find a way in which the tragic conundrum or paradox of needless unemployment can be overcome without the loss of political or economic freedom. We must provide for full employment after the physical wars have been won.

The National Debt *does* matter. Policies cannot be pursued indefinitely by deficit spending. Even though — as it has been said — we owe the debt to ourselves, to our own people, what is paid in interest becomes income to someone else — *the creators and lenders of debt.* Though all the people must pay it, it is owed to a comparative few.

The servicing of the debt will require the payment of billions upon billions of needless dollars in taxes by every family, rich or poor, in the whole country. The larger the interest-bearing National Debt, the greater will be the problem of securing the distribution of buying power among the people to make full production and full employment possible. So the road to an ever-increasing National Debt is a road that leads to an economy more and more centralized in the hands of the few.

There is a limit to the proportion of its income that any nation can afford to pay *in needless interest* to the holders of its bonds. There is a limit to the tax burden that the American people can and will willingly bear.

No political party or group can expect to hold the support of the American electorate unless it can furnish that electorate some answer other than oratory to the problems of unemployment and the public debt. There must be jobs for returning soldiers and there must be full employment and opportunity for abundant consumption for all after war if we would protect our liberties with something other than constant "deficit financing" by government "borrowing-at-interest" of privately created credit and a consequent increase in the National Debt *that-ought-not-to-be-debt.*

There must be a better, sounder, more solid basis for full employment and an equally abundant economy than we have as yet laid down. Full employment, abundant production and equally abundant consumption can be achieved without economic dictatorship or government control of our economy. The job of government must be the motivation of full employment and production — in peacetime as well as in war — by government regularly passing its power on into the hands of the people of the nation.

The first line of economic defense should be to make certain that American consumers will have a constant buying power large enough in total volume to keep our machinery of productions going at a high enough level to provide employment to everyone who wants to and needs to work.

The more the products of a nation such as the United States it can ship away to other lands the better off it is. A **scientific, interest-free monetary system** such as this book describes would guarantee to its people, as a whole, the constant ability to consume as much and more than they could produce. This guarantee would remove the fear of imports which would bless a nation living under the false delusion that an abundance of goods causes unemployment and that unemployment is to be cured by reducing the supply of goods and services, instead of increasing effective demand.

The price of enduring peace is, first of all, the removal from the path of international trade the barrier of **uncollectible and needless debt,** by founding trade upon the principle of an equal exchange of services and goods among and between the peoples of the world.

Only when the domestic seller and foreign seller can be sure when he is paid in dollars that he is receiving money that will constantly buy the same quantity of American goods from year to year, will we have a rock upon which to build a trade that will make for a lasting peace and supply the world with the necessities of life.

6
Implications of HJR 192 of 1933

On April 5, 1933, then president Franklin Delano Roosevelt, under Executive Order, declared that: "All persons are required to deliver ON OR BEFORE MAY 1, 1933, ALL GOLD COIN, GOLD BULLION, AND GOLD CERTIFICATES now owned by them to a Federal Reserve Bank, branch or agency, or to any member bank of the Federal Reserve System."

James A. Farley, Postmaster General at that time, required each postmaster in the country to post a copy of the Executive Order in a conspicuous place within each branch of the Post Office. On the bottom of the posting was the following:

CRIMINAL PENALTIES FOR VIOLATION OF EXECUTIVE ORDER a $10,000 fine or 10 years imprisonment, or both, as provided in Section 9 of the order.

Section 9 of the order reads as follows:

"Whosoever willfully violates any provisions of this Executive Order or of these regulations or of any rule, regulation or license issued thereunder may be fined not more than $10,000, or if a natural person, may be imprisoned for not more than 10 years, or both; and any officer, director or agency of any corporation who knowingly participates in any such violation may be punished by a like fine, imprisonment, or both."

NOTE: Stated within a written document received September 17, 1997, from the U.S. Department of Justice, Office of Legal Counsel, Office of the Deputy Assistant Attorney General, Richard L. Shiffin, in response to a FOIA, was the following:

"A fact that is frequently overlooked is that Executive orders and proclamations of the President normally have no direct effect upon *private persons or their property,* and instead, normally constitute only directives or instructions to officers or *employees of the Federal Government.*

"The exception is those cases in which the President is expressly authorized, or required by laws enacted by the Congress, to issue an Executive order or proclamation dealing with the legal rights or obligations of members of the public. Such as issuance of Selective Service Regulations, establishment of boards to investigate certain labor disputes, and establishment of quotas or fees with respect to certain imports into this country."

NOTE: IT SEEMS RATHER OBVIOUS THAT PRESIDENT FRANKLIN D. ROOSEVELT WAS NOT "EXPRESSLY AUTHORIZED OR REQUIRED" TO "ISSUE AN EXECUTIVE ORDER OR PROCLAMATION" DEMANDING THE PUBLIC TO RELINQUISH THEIR PRIVATELY HELD GOLD.

The order (the proclamation) issued by Roosevelt **was an undisciplined act of treason.**

Two months AFTER the Executive Order of June 5, 1933,

the Senate and House of Representatives, 73d Congress, 1st session, at 4:30 p.m. approved **House Joint Resolution 192: Joint Resolution To Suspend The Gold Standard And Abrogate The Gold Clause, Joint resolution to assure uniform value to the coins and currencies of the United States.**

[See HJR 192 of 1933 in APPENDIX]

HJR-192 states, in part, that "every provision contained in or made with respect to any obligation which purports to give the obligee a right to require payment in gold or a particular kind of coin or currency, or in any amount of money of the United States measured thereby, is declared to be against public policy, and no such provision shall be contained in or made with respect to any obligation hereafter incurred. **Every obligation**, heretofore or hereafter incurred, whether or not any such provisions is contained therein or made with respect thereto, **shall be discharged upon payment, dollar for dollar, in any such coin or currency which at the time of payment is legal tender** for public and private debts."

HJR-192 goes on to state: "As used in this resolution, the term 'obligation' means an obligation (including every obligation of and to the United States, excepting currency) payable in money of the United States; and the term 'coin or currency' means coin or currency of the United States, including Federal Reserve notes and circulating notes of Federal Reserve banks and national banking associations."

HJR-192 superseded Public Law (what passes as law today is only "color of law"), replacing it **with Public Policy**. **This eliminated our ability to PAY our debts, allowing only for their DISCHARGE. When we use any commer-

cial paper (checks, drafts, warrants, federal reserve notes, etc.), and accept it as money, ***we simply pass the unpaid debt attached to the paper on to others, by way of our purchases and transactions.*** This unpaid debt, under public policy, now carries a public liability for its collection. In other words, ***all debt is now public debt.***

The United States government, in order to provide necessary goods and services, **created a commercial bond** (promissory note), **by pledging the property, labor, life and body of its citizens, as payment for the debt** (bankruptcy). **This commercial bond made chattel** (property) **out of every man, woman and child in the United States.** We became nothing more than *"human resources"* and collateral for the debt. **This was without our knowledge and/or our consent.**

How was it done? It was done through the filing (registration) **of our birth certificates!**

The United States government — actually the elected and appointed administrators of government — took (and still does to this day) certified copies of all our birth certificates and placed them in the United States Department of Commerce ... as registered securities. These securities, each of which carries an estimated $1,000,000 (one million) dollar value, have been (and still are) circulated around the world as collateral for loans, entries on the asset side of ledgers, etc., just like any other security.

There's just one problem, we didn't authorize it.

The United States is a District of Columbia corporation. ***"The United States government is a foreign corporation with respect to a State"*** — Volume 20: Corpus Juris

Sec. § 1785 (see: NY re: Merriam 36 N.E. 505 1441 S. 0.1973, 14 L. Ed. 287).

Since a corporation is a fictitious "person" that cannot speak, see, touch, smell, etc., it cannot, by itself, function in the real world. It needs a conduit, **a transmitting utility,** a liaison of some sort, to "connect" the fictional person, and fictional world in which it exists, to the real world.

Why is this important?

Because LIVING people exist in the *real world,* not in a fictional world. But government exists in a *fictional world,* and can only deal directly with other fictional persons, agencies, states, corporations, etc. In order for a fictional person to deal with *real people* there must be a connection, a liaison, a go-between. This can be something as simple as a commercial contract.

When both "persons," the real and the fictional, agree to the terms of a contract, there is a *connection, intercourse, dealings,* there is a *communication,* an *exchange;* there is *business!*

But there is another way for fictional government to deal with real people: through the use of a *representative,* a *liaison,* a *go-between.* Who is this *representative?* This *liaison* that connects fictional government to real women and men? It's a government created *shadow,* a *fictional strawman* ... with the same name as ours.

This artificial PERSON was created by using our birth certificates as its MCO (Manufacturer's Certificate of Origin) and the state in which we were born as its "Port of Entry." This gave fictional government an artificial PERSON to deal with directly. This PERSON is our mirror image Strawman.

STRAMINEUS HOMO: Latin: A man of straw, one of no substance **put forward as bail** or surety. This definition comes from *Black's Law Dictionary, 6th. Edition, page 1421.* Following the definition of STRAMINEUS HOMO in Black's we find the next word, Strawman.

STRAWMAN: A front, a third party who is put up in name only to take part in a transaction. Nominal party to a transaction; one who acts as an *agent for another* for the purposes of taking title to real property and executing whatever documents and instruments the principal may direct. A person who purchases property for another to conceal identity of the real purchaser or to accomplish some purpose otherwise not allowed.

Webster's Ninth New Collegiate Dictionary defines the term "STRAWMAN" as:
 1: A weak or imaginary opposition set up only to be easily confuted
 2: A person set up to serve as a cover for a usually questionable transaction.

The Strawman can be summed up as an imaginary, *passive stand-in* for the real participant; a front; a blind; a person regarded as a nonentity. The Strawman is a *"shadow" go-between.*

For quite some time a rather large number of people in this country have known that a man or woman's name, written in ALL CAPS, or last name first, does not identify real, living people. Taking this one step further, the rules of grammar for the English language have no provisions for the abbreviation of people's names, i.e. initials are not to be used.

As an example, John Adam Smith is correct. *ANYTHING* else is not correct. Not Smith, John Adam or Smith, John A. or J. Smith or J. A. Smith or JOHN ADAM SMITH or SMITH, JOHN or any other variation. *NOTHING*, other than John Adam Smith identifies the real, living man. All other appellations identify either a *deceased* man or a *fictitious* man: such as a corporation or STRAWMAN.

Over the years government, through its "public" school system, has managed to pull the wool over our eyes and keep us ignorant of some very important facts. Because all facets of the media (print, radio, television) have an ever-increasing influence in our lives, and because media is controlled by government and its agencies, with the issuance of licenses, etc., we have slowly and systematically been conditioned to believe that any form or appellation of our names is, in fact, still us: as long as the spelling is correct. WRONG!

We were never told, with full and open disclosure, what our government officials were planning to do ... and why.

We were never told that the United States government is a corporation, a fictitious "person."

We were never told that our government had quietly, almost secretly, created a fictional shadow, a STRAWMAN, for each and every AMERICAN . . . so that the government could not only "control" us, the people, but also raise an unlimited amount of revenue so it could continue, not just to exist, but to GROW.

We were never told that when our government deals with the STRAWMAN it is not dealing with us, the real, living people.

We were never told — openly and clearly with full disclosure of all the facts — that we have been unable to pay our debts since June 5, 1933.

We were never told that we have been pledged (and our children, and their children, and their children, and on and on) as collateral, mere chattel, for the debt created by government officials who committed treason when they did.

We were never told that they quietly and cleverly changed the rules, even the game itself, and that the world we perceive as real is in fact fictional, and it's all for their benefit.

We were never told that the STRAWMAN, a fictional person, a creature of the state, is subject to all the codes, statutes, rules, regulations, ordinances, etc. decreed by government, but that we, the real women and men, are not.

We were never told that we were being treated as property, as indentured servants (albeit comfortably for some), while living in the land of the free, and that we could easily walk away from the fraud.

We were never told we were being abused!

There's something else you should know:

Everything since June 1933 operates in commerce!
Why is this important?

Because **commerce is based on contracts.** The government has an *implied contract* with the strawman (government's creation) whereby the strawman is subject to government rule.

When we step into their commercial process we become the "surety" for the fictional Strawman. Reality and fiction are reversed.

We become liable for the debts, liabilities and obligations of the strawman and relinquish our real, protected character as we stand in the place of our fictional strawman.

The fictional government can only function in a fictional commercial world, where **there is no real money,** only fictional funds ... mere *entries, figures, digits.*

A presentment from a fictional corporation — from a traffic citation to a criminal charge — is a negative "claim" against the strawman. This "claim" takes place in the fictional world of government. "Digits" move from one side of your strawman's account to the other — or to a different account. This is today's commerce.

In the past we addressed such "claims" by fighting them in court with one "legal process" after another and failed. We played the futile, legalistic, "dog-and-pony show," while the commerce game played on.

But what if we refuse to play the "dog-and-pony show"? What if we play the commerce game instead? What if we "go with the flow" instead of fighting the system. **What if we use the system** ourselves **instead.** Why not Accept their presentments for Value and extinguish their claims?

This is the power of commercial contracts.
And it should be mentioned at least this one time:

A contract overrides the Constitution, the Bill of Rights, and any other document other than another contract.

No process of law can operate upon you, no agent or agency of government, including the courts, can gain jurisdiction over you, WITHOUT YOUR CONSENT. You are not in their fictional domain unless you volunteer to be.

Money Doesn't Grow On Trees

The Accepted For Value process gives us the ability to deal with "them" through our transmitting utility strawman.

Yes. This process is effective. It can set you free from government oppression and control.
But remember: What goes around; comes around.
Do unto others as you would have others do unto you.

DO NOT ABUSE THIS PROCESS. It could come 'round and bite you in the end.

7
Money Without Debt

The money system of the Roman Republic was a money system created without debt to the government and to the people who pay its bills via taxes and the IRS.

Without the use of gold or silver, Rome became Mistress of the commerce of the world. Her people were the bravest, the most prosperous, and most happy, for they knew no grinding poverty. Her money was issued directly by the government and was composed of a cheap material — copper and brass — based alone upon the faith and credit of the people of the nation.

With this abundant money supply she built her magnificent temples and courts and other public structures. She distributed her lands among the people in small holdings, and wealth poured into the coffers and treasury of Rome.

But, then, Julius Caesar changed the money supply drastically. He began making gold coins with his image on them and declared himself Emperor of Rome for life putting an end to Rome's great experiment in *elected government* called a Republic.

Gold coins have always been the money of the rich.

The representatives in the Senate hated gold money and the Plutocracy (rule by the rich) that gold money implies.

Although the Senate assassinated Julius Caesar gold money had now taken root supported by the very rich and the Dictators they were able to buy with their gold.

After Julius Caesar was assassinated copper and brass coins were demonetized and removed from circulation and the quantity of available money was reduced by 90%.

A deep depression set in, like today. The average person had to sell his property in order to just buy the necessities of life. The wealth of the nation was quickly consolidated in the hands of the wealthiest Romans once again. Gone was the incentive for the common good.

Then Rome was sacked by the Visigoths and humanity was plunged into the dark ages.

With cheap government issued money the Roman Republic flourished but with gold money it perished.

This controversy between cheap money and gold money continues throughout history and is symbolized in part by the yellow brick road in the Wizard of Oz.

In 1100 A.D., in England, there were no banks like we think of them today. The goldsmiths controlled the economy of the nation, and even the monarchy. By acting together, the goldsmiths could either make money plentiful or scarce. When they made gold money plentiful the economy of the nation flourished, but when they made gold money scarce depression set in, and they could buy up the assets of the distressed people for pennies on the dollar.

About 100 A.D. King Henry I, son of England's first Norman King, William the Conqueror, was low on gold money. A series of costly wars had depleted the treasury so Henry created a unique form of government created money called tally sticks — polished sticks of wood (usually hazel wood) issued by the government, by the king, for the payment of taxes. This made wooden tally sticks just as good as any other form of money for the payment of debts.

This effective *debt free money system* lasted for more that seven hundred years. Without *needless* debt, England flourished into the greatest power on earth for centuries. At its peak more than 95% of England's money was in the form of tally sticks. Today the only form of *debt free government issued money* is in the form of coins. About 3% in the United Kingdom and far less than that in the United States.

After democratizing the money power of the nation with tally sticks, King Henry then decentralized political power itself. Then came the Charter of Liberties — followed by the Magna Charta in 1215. A merchant class began to develope.

In 1265, the first Parliamentarian elections were held. Government by the people in England was born, and in 1600 serfdom was legally banned. Humanity in England was finally set free. And the Bank of England was founded in 1694.

Simple sticks of wood broke the debt money system of England.

Every dollar in circulation today is an interest bearing debt created by the government by selling interest bearing IOUs to the private non-federal Federal Reserve Bank.

Americans are being robbed blind and they don't even know whose doing the robbing. The problem that's driving the economy into the ground is **needless debt** supported and allowed by the Congress of the United States.

When government spends more than it collects in taxes, it has be borrow the difference by selling interest bearing IOUs, such as interest bearing bonds, to the private non-federal Federal Reserve Bank.

When a US bank buys a $100 US interest bearing bond from the private non-federal Federal Reserve Bank, it gets to loan out *ten times that amount,* so the bank not only gets back the $100 plus interest from the Federal Government, it gets to loan our another $1000 it creates out of thin air, and charge additional interest on it in addition to receiving back the $1000 it created out of nothing in repayment of the loans it made to others.

The bank is *really* making about 1000% interest on that simple $100 deposit! ($100 at 5% = $105 x 10 more $100 loans = $1050/$100 = 1050% interest).

This is why bank buildings are the biggest buildings in town on the planet.

This system of *lending way more than you have* is called fractional reserve lending (FRL).

All of our money is created by banks lending *money and thin air* to people, companies or to the government. While the government could simply issue its money debt-free, itself, instead of borrowing it from the Federal Reserve Bank.

Simply issue it itself debt-free for the benefit of all the people equally. Abraham Lincoln did it, others did it. But the government is "in bed with" (in partnership with) the private non-federal Federal Reserve Bank.

"In our debt money system someone has to borrow every dollar we have in circulation. If the banks create ample money we are prosperous; if not, we starve. When one gets a complete grasp of the picture, the tragic absurdity of our hopeless position will be seen as incredible. It is the most important subject intelligent persons can investigate and reflect upon." — *1934, Robert H. Hemphill, Credit Manager of the Federal Reserve Bank of Atlanta.*

The government doesn't need to go into debt, it can issue all the money it needs itself.

What government officials can't raise from taxes they borrow from banks.

An Oligarchy is a group of powerful people who have hijacked the United States Government by going into partnership with the private non-federal Federal Reserve Bank.

You can't borrow yourself out of debt, and no one is talking about the debt system that enslaves the people.

The solution to this problem of debt is not new.

The government should take charge of the money supply; all that matters is who controls its QUANTITY.

8
The Money Issue

In 1907, a money panic occurred which many believed to be caused by deliberate international gold shipments which depleted bank reserves.

As a result of the damage caused by this money panic, the people of our nation, and various politicians, agitated for monetary reform. Paul Warburg, who immigrated from Germany to our country in 1902 — who was an officer of the banking firm of Kuhn Loeb and Company — proposed a great Central Bank in the European tradition. Congress established a monetary commission to study this proposal, and many of the commission's reports can now be found in Senate and House Documents of that period.

In 1909, the 16th Amendment to the U.S. Constitution, establishing the income tax, was proposed and supposedly ratified in February, 1913. The income tax was a condition precedent for a fiat currency system. Between 1909 and 1913, the plan for the proposed central bank took shape; and the Federal Reserve Act, establishing the private non-federal Federal Reserve System of Banks was passed December 23, 1913.

The Federal Reserve Act, as sold to the American public by its proponents, gave the outward appearance that the "Money Trust" was being destroyed and replaced by a government agency which would operate for the benefit of the people. The people were defrauded because the Act did not dethrone the "Money Trust" but in fact granted vast and unknown powers to it.

Private groups have always desired to have the power to provide currency to a nation and this act in fact gave Congress' power to issue legal tender Treasury notes to a powerful, private financial group of men.

The Federal Reserve Act established 12 privately owned Federal Reserve Banks, whose stock was to be owned by the member banks. These 12 private regional central banks comprise the system now known as the Federal Reserve Bank. The only public attribute of this System is that it is controlled by a 12 member Board of Governors, 7 of whom are appointed by the President of the United States.

The System is totally private, having only a few titular "public" heads. The financial powers that sought and obtained this legislation desired a privately owned system with enough public facade which gives the deceptive appearance of government authority. Not only does legislation disclose the private nature of this System, the federal courts have recognized this fact; see *Lewis v. United States*, 680 F.2d 1239 (9th Cir. 1982).

The original act authorized the issuance of Federal Reserve Notes which were to be redeemed in "lawful money of the United States," according to 12 USC 411.

And 12 USC 152, prior to its repeal in 1994, defined "lawful money" to be gold and silver coin. Therefore the act called for "specie redemption" of such notes. The fact that such notes were deemed to be "obligations of the United States" shows conclusively that Congress' power to issue legal tender Treasury notes — derived from its power to **"borrow money on the credit of the United States"** (Article 1, Section 8, clause. 1) — was "given" to the System.

Because the Federal Reserve Act conveyed this very substantial Congressional power to a private banking cartel, the question arises concerning the constitutionality of this legislation.

It is not necessary to consider the infinite numerous transactions of the System — such as its open market operations, discount operations and flagrant, abusive, tortious manipulations of the reserve requirement ratio — since the only crucial link to Congress' power to issue legal tender Treasury notes is the fact that Federal Reserve Notes are obligations of the United States payable back to the Federal Reserve.

Since Congress established no discernible purpose or policy, insofar as the issuance of these obligations is concerned, there is no standard by which the actions of the private System can be controlled. There are no rules, regulations, or procedures to be followed concerning the issuance of these FRNs. There are no requirements for findings of fact regarding the issuance of FRNs, no administrative procedures, such as public hearings and the opportunity to be publicly heard.

The conveyance of Congressional power, to issue legal tender Treasury notes to these banks, was an outright gift to a very powerful, self interested financial cartel, subject to no restraint or control by Congress. The Federal Reserve System was given *unbridled power* to expand or contract the quantity and worth of outstanding federal "bills of credit." This legislation is unconstitutional for this very fact, and was the first step in the complete take-over of the United States and the funding of the First World War.

The Federal Reserve System was established just in time for the war, the System created all the credit needed to finance that war. Federal bonds were sold to the Federal Reserve Bank in exchange for credit to the government for federal bonds. These federal bonds — *public* promissory notes — became the basis upon which Federal Reserve Notes — **private** promissory notes — were issued.

Public promises were used to borrow the private Credit of the American people from the private, non-federal, Federal Reserve Bank.

So as the war progressed, the U.S. currency and credit supply greatly expanded, directly causing inflation.

After the conclusion of the war, the Federal Reserve System intentionally *contracted* the currency supply. The Federal Reserve had demonstrated its ability to *expand* the currency supply, now it was time to test its ability to *contract* it. On May 18, 1920, a secret meeting of the Federal Reserve Board devised a *criminal plan* to severely damage the commerce of the United States, the agriculture industry in particular.

During this meeting, plans were made to severely raise the reserve requirements and discount rate. The results were predictable, and agriculture and its support industries received a severe financial blow, all for the purpose of reducing food prices. Great financial ruin resulted and those who were damaged were without fault. The System proved to be efficient at *contracting the money supply,* thus laying the groundwork for the Great Depression.

After this *vicious* and *criminal* currency contraction, the System began the inflationary policy that created the bubble of the "roaring twenties." By 1926, 1927, and 1928, newspapers, bank officials, stockbrokers, and even the President and Governors of the states praised the "good times" and encouraged people to enter the stock market because "prosperity had now arrived."

But during the spring or summer of 1929, plans similar to those devised on May 18, 1920 were seen to be operating, and on October 29, 1929, the speculation bubble — caused by the inflationary policy of the "Fed" — broke, and the Great Depression of our nation began. Fortunes are made by *inflationary currency policies* and *contractional currency policies* as well. The trick is to know when the effect of these policies will occur; those in the know made fortunes during the Depression, compliments of the System created and allowed by Congress.

While the Great Depression was caused by the contraction of currency and credit, the Federal Reserve System had been given the ability to *create credit without limit.* The System withdrew credit from the private sector of our economy to cause the Depression, but between the collapse in October, 1929, and June 1, 1933, the Federal Reserve Banks' ability to create credit enabled it to use the private credit it stole from the American people to buy federal bonds redeemable in gold.

By June 1, 1933, the Federal Reserve System held virtually all of the United States gold bonds that were to mature between June 1, 1933, and January 1, 1934.

Owning these bonds put the Federal Reserve in a position to dictate the fate of the nation to Congress, and these private non-federal Federal Reserve Banks did exactly that, and have been doing so ever since!

GIVE YOURSELF CREDIT

9
Follow Through

On March 4, 1933, Franklin Roosevelt was inaugurated U.S. President at a very troubling time in the Depression.

On March 6, 1933, Roosevelt declared a banking holiday and closed the doors of the nation's banks, on the authority of the expired, World War I Trading With the Enemy Act, 40 Stat. 411, which had expired at the termination of that War, to authorize the President to outlaw the hoarding of gold. Some of the banks that were closed as a result of Roosevelt's Executive Order never reopened, to the ruin of their depositing customers.

Roosevelt called an emergency session of Congress for March 9, 1933. When the House convened, it immediately passed the Emergency Banking Act of 1933 without seeing a copy of the proposed legislation and with only 40 minutes debate. The United States was bankrupt and the Receivers were in charge behind the scenes. Never before or since has a piece of legislation been "railroaded" as this one was, until the present time.

A similar railroad move took place in the Senate. And at the end of the day, Roosevelt's after-the-fact approval of his legislative act, which closed the banks, became law. In addition, this new law enabled the Secretary of the Treasury to take over all of the private gold in the United States.

Roosevelt extended the bank holiday with his new powers and issued another Executive Order on March 10, 1933, to divest Americans of their constitutional right to possess gold. Thus commenced the war on gold initiated by the American President at that time.

By June 1, 1933, Congressional Joint Resolution 192 was proposed to make it against Public Policy to pay any obligation in gold.

During the debate on this resolution the fact was made known that the Federal Reserve Bank owned all the federal gold-clause bonds maturing the next 6 months. (Congressional Record, June 1, 1933, page 4899). The Federal United States was bankrupt.

House Joint Resolution 192 was enacted on June 5, 1933, and even though it was only a *resolution,* it was given the force of law.

On August 28, 1933, Roosevelt issued another Executive Order which required "Information Returns" for gold ownership and outlawed the ownership of gold without a license. Failure to file the return, and owning gold without license, were made crimes against the state. Roosevelt's legislation to outlaw gold made the federal government the biggest "hoarder" of gold in the world, and put America on the "inconvertible currency" - "promissory note" standard, instead of the "gold" standard that America had been on before.

This "inconvertible currency" - "promissory note" standard was deemed "modern" like the architecture of the 1930s and the "boat tail" Duesenbergs, Auburns, and Cords.

The final piece of legislation Roosevelt secured in his war on the ownership of gold by American citizens was the Gold Reserve Act of January 30, 1934, 48 Stat. 337. This legislation was *also* railroaded through Congress in the manipulative tradition used to obtain the Emergency Banking Act of 1933. Roosevelt and Congress used an alleged "National Emergency" (actually, the bankruptcy of the federal United States) as the predicate for the hasty legislation and orders so issued.

10
Orchestrated Results

Since the changes in the monetary system of the 1930s, the federal government has unilaterally ceased to fulfill its monetary responsibilities required by the Constitution and has *allowed the critical function of providing currency to the nation* to be usurped by the Federal Reserve Banks. The minting of dollars of silver ceased in the 1930s, and the gold reserves, so violently taken from the American people, were used to support greater and greater quantities of notes as the gold reserve requirement was lowered over a span of many years.

The vacuum created by Congressional nonfeasance, or malfeasance — insofar as the currency system is concerned — enabled the Federal Reserve System to play a greater and greater role in providing currency. This favorable environment followed directly as a result of this System *proving its ability* to bankrupt the federal government by the gold bonds it held immediately prior to June 5, 1933.

The open question is whether the Federal Reserve System did in fact have the gold required to pay the gold bonds the System held at that time. A possible answer to this question seems to lie in the fact that the Federal Reserve Bank of New York had or has many tons of gold in its possession beneath the streets of New York City and the further fact that the Federal Reserve claims a lien upon or title to all the gold the government possessed.

Since the debacle of the 1930s, the "Fed" has provided monumental amounts of "credit" to the Federal Government to finance World War II, the Korean War, and the vast increase in social programs enacted by Congress. The increasing quantities of "credit" provided to the Federal Government has enabled it to acquire more and more control over the GNP of our nation.

On the day President Kennedy was buried, when the country was looking the other way, the first *irredeemable* Federal Reserve Notes were shipped out from the United States Treasury.

Shortly thereafter, the Treasury consulted Merrill Jenkins, a nationally renown expert on vending machines, to determine how "slugs" could be used to operate vending machines; Jenkins suggested a "sandwiched" coin. Thereafter, President Johnson used the media to promote the idea of a silver shortage, and soon clad coins came into circulation pursuant to the Coinage Act of 1965, 79 Stat. 254.

Once debased clad-coins had been provided to the nation by the Treasury, the one remaining step necessary to put the nation itself on the fiat, *irredeemable promissory note standard* was to prevent redemption of circulating notes with silver. This came in 1967 with the Silver Certificate Act, 81 Stat. 77, which provided that redemption of silver certificates would end on June 24, 1968.

The very next day, on June 25, 1968, the nation was placed on a completely fiat, *irredeemable promissory note standard* standard. Since then, the nation has been floating upon a "vast commercial sea" of paper currency and credit, and red ink.

11
Conditions Now

If any crime against the law and mankind has ever occurred, it was surely the crime that Congress committed when it established the Federal Reserve System in 1913. This act created 12 privately owned banks of issue which were unified into one private System and given a public facade for appearance sake. For no consideration, and without any restraints being placed upon the Grant, Congress empowered these banks to issue notes which were deemed to be obligations of the federal United States Government in behalf of the people.

After creation, these banks quickly assumed a prominent position in the financial affairs of this nation, which they have held ever since. Their power was exercised adversely in 1920 and 1921, and the result was a depression in agriculture. Thereafter, these banks created a boom which, when the bubble burst, ended in the worst economic calamity known to modern man, to date, the Great Depression.

During the Depression, these banks made war against the UNITED STATES.

Gold and silver coins have always been and always will be the enemy of paper money. The friends of paper money, during this dark era in our history, made certain that gold would never again offend them; the embarrassing predicament in which they placed the federal government was sufficient to cause the federal government to take an action unprecedented in the annals of the history of money. This action was the bold move to confiscate all gold in the possession of private American citizens and, allegedly, to forever lock it up in the vaults of Fort Knox. All of this occurred during a "National Emergency" that was the predicate for the actions taken.

The knowledge and experience gained by the central bankers in the 30's was put to use in the 60's when a very silent war against silver was conducted, which resulted in the obliteration of all connections between this precious metal and our currency. While the attention of the American public was focused upon the preparations for sending men to the moon, one of the deadliest social diseases ever known to man — fiat money — was introduced to our nation.

Today, the currency system in our country is totally privately owned and controlled; it is manipulated at will and is specifically designed to financially conquer the people of America. The chief bank note which this system issues, the FRN, is totally irredeemable. These notes, in addition to credit claims against the Federal Reserve Bank, constitute the reserves upon which the nation's private banks issue a multiple of demand deposits out of thin air, which are likewise irredeemable. The issue of the FRNs of all these private banks is plainly unconstitutional. And this entire system has been imposed upon the American people with irresistible force and the power of the gun.

Our entire currency system is as unconstitutional as the Confederate currency system was of Civil War times.

Since the advent of fiat paper money, our nation has suffered from the identical ills which the Framers of the Constitution endured and sought to prevent. Inflation is endemic, taxes are constantly rising, crime is rampant, Americans are unemployed and loosing their homes at a deplorable rate, and that great institution, the American family, is falling apart. These are always the direct social consequences whenever any nation has permitted its currency to be debauched, as history has clearly shown.

Neither the national executive or legislative branches display any inclination, nor their lawful authority, to remedy this severe social problem. Further, state governors and legislators are afflicted with a supposed lack of knowledge of the true nature of coin, credit, and monetary circulation and are therefore *unable* or *unwilling* to offer redress.

However, the judiciary of our nation *does* offer hope and has given the people a ready REMEDY that they can implement to revitalize America . . .

The perfect solution lawfully established in HJR 192 of 1933.

12
How Banks Operate

It is well recognized by banking textbooks and experts that banks engage in a practice known as **"deposit creation,"** which, in essence, is simply the creation of credit by bookkeeping entry. As the Federal Reserve Bank of Chicago has so aptly stated in its publication, *Modern Money Mechanics:*

> "The actual process of money creation takes place in the banks. As noted earlier, checkable liabilities of banks are money. These liabilities are **customers' accounts**. They **increase when the customers deposit currency and checks and when** the **proceeds of loans** made by the banks **are credited to borrowers' accounts**.
>
> "In the absence of legal reserve requirements, **banks** can **build up deposits by increasing loans and investments** so long as they keep enough currency on hand to redeem whatever amounts the holders of deposits want to convert into currency."

Thus, **banks simply extend "credit"** when loans are made. The **"currency"** for which these and all other loans in America **can be redeemed** is known **as Federal Reserve Notes** ("FRNs").

The **reserves** held by Federal Reserve Banks **have been**

Money Doesn't Grow On Trees

admitted by the government in its work titled *A Primer on Money* **to be "backed" by nothing**:

"Today, the American people use coins, **currency** (**paper money**), and commercial bank **demand deposits** (**checkbook money**)," Id., at 17.

"The private commercial banks issue 'checkbook money.

"Imagine there is only one bank in the country and that it has two private depositors, each with $50 in his checking account. Total bank demand deposits would then be $100. Suppose John Jones asked for a $50 loan from the bank, and the bank approved the loan. **The bank would then lend the money to Mr. Jones by simply opening a checking account for him** and depositing $50 in it. This is what ordinarily happens **when anyone**— business or private individual— **borrows from a bank**. **The bank deposits** the amount of **the loan** in the relevant checking account.

"**In making the loan** to Mr. Jones, **the bank** did not reduce anyone's previous bank balance. It simply **credited the Jones account with $50**. The total amount held in bank **demand deposits now becomes $150**. **The bank** has, therefore, **issued $50 in 'checkbook money**.'

"The natural question to ask is, **Where does the bank get the additional $50** to issue and lend to Mr. Jones? The answer, as will become clear in the next chapter, is that the bank did not 'get' the money at all. **The money has been created**," Id. at 19-20.

"**All money** used in this country and in most countries of the world **is of two types**. One is **'printing press money,'** which is money printed by the Government. The other type of money in use is **'pen-and-ink money.'** Pen-and-ink money is **created** by the private commercial banks **each time a bank makes a loan**, buys a U.S. Government security, **or buys any** other **asset**. Printing press money is engraved on special paper and with special inks; and it costs about 1 cent per bill, whether a $1 bill or a $10,000 bill. **Pen-and-ink money is created by** a private banker simply by making ink marks on the books of the bank. However, in recent years many of the banks have installed electronic office machines which make the **entries in the banks' books**; so someday we may come to refer to bank-created money as 'office machine money' or perhaps 'Univac money,'" Id., at 48-49.

"In the first place, **one of the major functions of** the private commercial **banks is to create money**. A large portion of bank profits come from the fact that the banks do create money. And, as we have pointed out, **banks create money without cost to themselves**, in the process of lending or investing in securities such as Government bonds. Bank profits come from interest on the money lent and invested, while the cost of creating money is negligible. (Banks do incur costs, of course, from bookkeeping to loan officers' salaries.) **The power to create money has been delegated**, or loaned, **by**

Congress to the private banks for their free use. There is no charge," Id., at 89.

"Since I had also seen **reports that** the **member banks** of the Federal Reserve System **have** a certain number of millions of dollars in **'cash reserves' on deposit with the Federal Reserve bank**, I then asked if I might be allowed to see these cash reserves. This time my question was met with some looks of surprise; the bank officials then patiently explained to me that **there are no cash reserves**. The **cash**, in truth, **does not exist** and never has existed. What are called **cash reserves are** simply **bookkeeping credits** entered into the ledgers of the Federal Reserve banks. These credits are first **created by the Federal Reserve** and then passed along through the banking system.

"On another occasion, in the spring of 1960, I paid a visit to the Federal Reserve Bank of Richmond, along with several other Members of Congress, and in the course of the visit asked the President of that bank if I could see the cash reserves which the member banks had on deposit with that bank. Here the answer was in substance the same. **There is no cash in the so-called cash reserves**. In other words, **the cash** making up the banks' 'cash reserves' with the Federal Reserve bank **is just a myth**," Id., at 38.

Mr. Russell Munk, an official employed at the United States Treasury Department, has declared that common **banking practices** today **involve** mere **extensions of credit via loans**:

"If the money supply is to be increased, **money must be created**. The Federal Reserve Board (or 'the Fed' as it is often called) has several ways of allowing money to be created, but the actual **creation of money** always **involves the extension of credit** by private commercial banks." [the credit of the people].

"In both the goldsmiths' practice and in modern banking, **new money is created by** offering **loans** to customers. **A private commercial bank** which has just received extra reserves from the Fed (by borrowing reserves for example) **can make roughly ten dollars in loans for every one dollar in reserves** it obtains from the Fed. **How does it** get ten dollars from one dollar? **It** simply **makes book entries** for its loan customers **saying "you have a deposit of ten dollars with us."**

Banks are prohibited by law from loaning *their assets* or *their customer's assets*.

Money Doesn't Grow On Trees

13
Balance Your Account

[Adapted from Lesson 18 of *New beginning Study Course*]

YOU ARE THE CREDITOR of your debtor strawman — whether you know it not.

Corporate entities are **pretending** to be creditors in your place. Why are they getting the *interest* of the credit that you have supplied to the corporations in the public domain?

The corporations should be paying the *interest* on your credit to you, instead to themselves.

How did this get switched around whereby the head is the tail and the tail is the head?

"The stranger that is within you shall get up above you very high; and you shall come down very low. He shall lend to you and you shall not lend to him; **he shall be the head, and you shall be the tail.** *Moreover all these curses shall come upon you, and shall pursue you, and overtake you, till you be destroyed;* **because you hearkened not unto the voice of the Lord your God,** *to keep his commandments and his statutes which he commanded you."* (Deut. 28:43, 44 & 45).

Countless "charges" have been entered against your corporate strawman without your knowledge or consent. What can you do about it?

You can balance your account by ACCEPTANCE FOR VALUE. You can *zero out* these accounts with your credit and discharge all other debts that you can see.

The United States Federal Government has been dissolved.

HJR 192, of June 5, 1933, "Joint Resolution To Suspend The Gold Standard and Abrogate The Gold Clause" completely dissolved the United States. The federal government of the United States exists today in name only.

The Receivers of the United States Bankruptcy are the International Bankers, via the United Nations, the World Bank and the International Monetary Fund.

All United States Offices, Officials, and Departments are now operating in name only under Emergency War Powers. The receivers of the Bankruptcy have adopted a new form of government for the United States. This new form is known as the Democracy. An established, Socialist/Communist New World Order, by transferring the Office of the Secretary of Treasury to that of the Governor of the International Monetary Fund.

Gold and silver were such a powerful money during the founding of the United States of America, that the founding fathers declared that only gold and silver coins can be "money" in America. And since gold and silver coins were heavy and inconvenient for a lot of transactions, they were stored in banks and claim checks were issued as money substitutes instead.

Federal Reserve Notes (FRN's) are not "money."

It is essential that we comprehend the difference between real money and a paper money substitutes. You cannot get rich by accumulating money substitutes, you only get deeper in debt.

We the People no longer have any "money" but we have our credit.

Federal Reserve Notes (FRN's) are unsigned checks written on a closed account.

FRN's are promissory notes promising to pay the national debt to the non-federal, Federal Reserve Bank.

To pay a debt, you must pay with value or substance (gold, silver, barter or a commodity). With FRN's, you can only discharge a debt.

You cannot pay a debt with a debt currency system. Minus $10 dollars, *minus* minus $10 dollars = minus $20 dollars.

No contract is valid unless it involves an exchange of "good and valuable consideration." Unpayable debt transfers power and control to the governors of the international banks.

The Federal Reserve System is patterned on a "Canon Law Trust"; adding stock and calling it a "Joint Stock Trust." The Federal Reserve is a sovereign power separate and distinct from the federal United States.

The Federal Reserve is a maritime *lender,* a maritime *insurance underwriter* to the federal United States operating exclusively under Admiralty/Maritime law.

The Federal Reserve Act stipulated that the *interest* on the national debt was to be paid in gold, but there was no stipulation that the *principle* ever had to be paid at all.

The Federal Reserve Act (1913) "hypothecated" all property in the federal United States to the Federal Reserve Bank. U.S. citizens (tenants, franchisees) were registered as "Beneficiaries" of the trust via their birth certificates.

In 1933, the federal United States hypothecated the present and future assets and labor of its "subjects" to the private non-federal Federal Reserve Bank.

In return, the Federal Reserve agreed to extend all the

Money Doesn't Grow On Trees

"credit" (money substitutes) it needed to the federal corporate United States. As with any debtor, the United States government had to assign collateral to its creditors as a condition of the loan.

Since the federal United States didn't have any assets, it assigned the private property of its "economic slaves" as collateral against the unpayable federal debt. It also pledged the unincorporated federal territories, the national forests and parks, all birth certificates, and all nonprofit organizations — such as churches and privately run schools — as collateral against the federal debt.

Everything has been transferred in payment to the international banks.

America has returned to its pre-American Revolution Feudal roots. We the People are Tenants renting our property from the Federal Reserve Bank.

We the People have exchanged one Master for another.

This has been going on ever since 1933, without the "informed" knowledge of the American people.

Why are 90% of Americans mortgaged to the hilt and have little or no assets after all debts and liabilities have been paid? Why does it feel like you are working harder and harder and receiving less and less?

We are reaping what we have sowed, and the result of the harvest is foreclosure — on American property, liberties, and way of life.

The federal United States is bankrupt — in world leadership, financial credit, vision and human rights.

This is an undeclared economic War . . . economic Slavery of the most corrupt kind !

14
Overcome Debt With Knowledge

[Adapted from Lesson 20 of *New beginning Study Course*]

Federal Reserve Notes are *promissory notes* that Congress *promises to redeem* with our credit, upon demand.

A bill is a demand for *real money:* currency backed by silver or gold. A bill is a demand for *payment* that can't be made because there is no *real money* with which to pay the charge.

Federal Reserve Notes in lieu of our credit discharge debt. Our credit (*our promises to pay*) will *extinguish* debt if we *accept the bill for its value with our credit sign* (our endorsement) to settle the account.

Congress borrows Federal Reserve Notes from the Federal Reserve Bank with bonds that accumulate interest for the Federal Reserve, **backed by the credit Congress borrows from us,** the People of America, making us preferred stockholders of the corporate UNITED STATES.

The *credit* that Congress borrows from us, the People of America, is called in the US Constitution *"the credit of the United States."*

In other words: The *credit* that Congress borrows is *"the credit of (the people that the people loan to) the United States."*

"Congress shall have power / to borrow money on the credit of the United States." — Article 1, Section 8, clause 2, U.S. Constitution. (1:8:2)

Congress borrows Federal Reserve Notes from the Federal Reserve Bank with bonds that are **backed by the credit of the American People.**

"Real money of account of the United States is currency backed by gold and silver coins manufactured in a United States Mint." (Coinage Act of 1792).

Federal Reserve Notes are *debt instruments* — evidences of debt that enslave us, *so why use them?* **The use of Federal Reserve Notes is voluntary.** Slavery to FRNs is an *optional choice, whether we know it or not.*

In 1933, House Joint Resolution 192 made it a federal offense to *refuse to accept* Federal Reserve Notes to discharge contract obligations demanding gold.

HJR 192 of 1933 did not *order* people to use Federal Reserve Notes to discharge debt — it *allowed* people to use Federal Reserve Notes to discharge debt.

People use FRNs *voluntarily, whether they know it or not.* By using FRNs, people *volunteer* into *voluntary servitude* to the Federal Reserve Bank.

Since there is no *real "money of account of the United States"* a charge (*an invoice; a bill*) is an *offer to contract* to settle the debt with Federal Reserve Notes or **a mutual offset credit exemption exchange.**

The Accepter has the option of *discharging* the debt with Federal Reserve Notes, or *paying* the debt with his *credit* — his **mutual offset credit exemption exchange** — if *knows that he can.*

Here is the **REMEDY**.
There is no real "money of account of the United States."

On May 23, 1933, Congressman Louis T. McFadden (R-OH), *Chairman of the House Banking and Finance Committee,* brought formal charges against the Federal Reserve Bank, the Comptroller of Currency and the Secretary of the Treasury of the United States, for numerous *criminal acts,* including FRAUD, UNLAWFUL CONVERSION OF MONEY, AND TREASON !

To protect themselves from these criminal charges the House and Senate passed House Joint Resolution 192 on June 5, 1933.

HJR 192 of 1933 stated that the people were exempt from paying their debts, since the *means of paying debts* had been taken away and replaced with Fiat paper Federal Reserve Notes that *discharge* debt instead of *paying* debt.

Public Insurance Policy HJR 192 of 1933 provided a REMEDY for the victims of President Roosevelt's crime. This REMEDY is the basis of lawful **mutual offset credit exemption exchange.**

This CONVERSION created the EXEMPTION upon which **mutual offset credit exemption exchange** is based.

The federal Government has been using the **UCC Contract Trust Account** in your name ever since you were born, **and keeping its interest,** *without your knowledge and consent,* to help pay the interest on the federal debt to the private non-federal Federal Reserve Bank.

The United States is the beneficiary of **a private constructive cestui que trust** and is using your *commercial energy* to fund the interest on its ever increasing national debt to the private non-federal Federal Reserve Bank.

The US Treasury created a *private constructive cestui que trust* through which the corporate United States and all its subsidiaries (*states, counties, cities, towns, school districts, fire districts, etc.*) interact with your *fictitious mirror image strawman.*

Fictions cannot interact with *living, flesh and blood women or men;* they can only interact with *fictitious, mirror image, strawmen,* that women and men are *presumed to accommodate* by co-signing agreements in their names.

The state has convinced you — *the living flesh and blood woman or man* — that it is addressing *you* instead of your fictional, e*ns legis, mirror image strawman. ("ens legis,"* means "legally created").

You are *presumed* to be voluntarily accommodating your *fictitious, mirror image strawman* whether you know it or not.

The *debt* belongs to the *fictitious* you, but the *real* you is *presumed* to be responsible for the *fictitious, mirror image strawman's* actions and debts.

Now that you are aware of this *presumption* **you can redeem your status by rebuttal** to recover *dollar for dollar* the collateral that the government has been holding in your name *and earning interest on* ever since you were born.

MAXIM: He who holds the gold pays the bills.

15
Commercial Redemption

In Commercial Redemption, a "presentment" (*an invoice or a bill, etc.*) is an offer to contract to discharge a debt.

A bill or a debt is a *negative charge* (*a debt*) to your debtor strawman but a *positive charge* (*an asset*) offered first to you, *the secured party creditor of your debtor strawman.*

It is NOT a demand for money from *you!* It is a payment of credit from your strawman *to you* because he is indebtedness to you *first.*

Everything is reversed.

A bill to your strawman is an offer of his credit to you *first* . . . so why not ACCEPT *credi offered,* and discharge the strawman's debt with a **mutual offset credit exemption exchange,** between you and the presenter, and settle and close the account?

To do this simply endorse the presentment your strawman received with your *signature* (*your credit sign*), and thereby acknowledge your acceptance of the *debt credit* for its value as a **mutual offset credit exemption exchange** that settles and closes the account.

Your *endorsement* of the charge with *your name* (*your signature*), *your number* (*your Social Security Number*), and *the date* transforms the charge into a *promissory note* that extinguishes the charge with a **mutual offset credit exemption exchange.**

The only money you have with which to extinguish a debt is your credit — *the constitutional credit of the United States* — via a **mutual offset credit exemption exchange.**

16
The Mark, The Name, The Number

[Chapter 33 of *Epistle to Americans II: about History*]

"AND *he causeth all, both small and great, free and bond, to receive a mark in their right hand, or in their foreheads: that no man might buy or sell, save he that had* **the mark**, *or* **the name** *of the beast, or* **the number** *of his name."* — Rev. 13:16,17.

2 "The mark, or the name of the beast" is the *trademark* or *tradename* of the *all capital letter strawman* that the government deals with directly instead of dealing with you.

3 Your strawman's *birthdate* on his birth certificate is the date when your *all capital letter government created trademark-tradename* was *berthed like a vessel,* by the State in your Port of Entry.

4 Your strawman's *trademark-tradename* doesn't belong to you; it belongs to your *artificial, vessel strawman.*

5 Your strawman's *birthdate* is the means by which you are *enticed* to be the *surety* for him — by which you are fooled into claiming *his* "berthdate" to be *yours.*

6 This is why you cannot speak for yourself in court. You must have a lawyer speak for you instead — *because you have told this lie.*

7 You *perjure yourself* when you state the date that you were born.

8 Evidence based on something that you were told is *hearsay*, and hearsay evidence is not recognized by the court.

9 Yes. You were physically present when you were born. But you were too young to know the date or the time first hand.

10 *To be acceptable, evidence must be witnessed to first hand.*

11 You also lie when you *"solemnly swear to tell the truth"*. Your *false birthdate claim* brings all of your subsequent testimony into question even when you profess to know and swear to tell the truth.

12 What's more: The government doesn't **want** you to tell the truth; it couldn't control you if you did.

13 **The government isn't based on truth; the government is based on agreement contracts.**

14 The "number of his name" is the *number* of your *strawman's name,* — the *number* of his *Social Security Account.*

15 You will find your strawman's *all capital letter, trademark-tradename* on his driver's license; on his bank account; on his telephone bills; on his power bills — on all the public papers that are addressed to your *government created, strawman*— not to you.

16 All of these *documents* that you think refer to you are not yours. These *documents* belong to your *ens legis fictional vessel strawman.*

17 **Welcome to the Wonderful World of Oz!**

17
Equity-Interest Recovery

[Chapter 51 of *Epistle to Americans III: about Money*]

DURING the financial crisis of the Great Depression of 1929-1933, the *tangible substance of real money* (*gold and silver*) was removed from the monetary system of the United States.

2 In its place the *intangible substance* of the American people (*the wealth and productivity that belongs to them*) was pledged by the government as collateral for the debt, credit, and currency of the UNITED STATES, and placed at risk so society's commerce could continue to function.

3 This is well documented in the actions of President Roosevelt and Congress and in the Congressional debates that preceded the execution of reorganization measures in bankruptcy.

4 *"The new money (paper Federal Reserve Substitutes for money) is issued to the banks in return for Government obligations, bills of exchange, drafts, notes, trade acceptance, and banker's acceptances. For example:*

5 *"**The new money** will be worth 100 cents on the dollar, because it **is backed by the credit of the nation.** (our credit).*

6 *"It will represent a mortgage on all the homes and other property of all the people in the nation. — Senate Document No. 43, 73rd Congress, 1st session.*

7 This new money belongs to *"all the people in the nation".*

8 The National Debt is defined as *"mortgages on the wealth and income of the people of the country." — Encyclopedia Britannica, 1959.*

9 The people's wealth is their income, physical energy, productivity, and private property.

10 The *bankruptcy reorganization* of the UNITED STATES is evidenced by (1) the Emergency Banking Act of March 9, 1933, (2) House Joint Resolution 192 of June 5, 1933, and (3) the Series of Presidential Executive Orders that surround them in 1933-34.

11 Twenty years prior to this on December 23, 1913, Congress passed *"An Act to Provide for the establishment of Federal Reserve Banks to furnish an Elastic Currency to afford a means of rediscounting Commercial Paper and to establish a more effective Supervision of banking in the United States **and for Other Purposes**"* — called The Federal Reserve Act.

12 One of the ***"Other purposes"*** of the Federal Reserve Act was to authorize the *hypothecation* of the obligations of the UNITED STATES which the Federal Reserve Banks were authorized to hold under 12 USC 14(a).

13 An *hypothecation* is a *"pledge of property as security or collateral for a debt without delivery of title or possession." — Federal Reserve Act, section 14(a).*

14 A *tacit hypothecation* is a hidden lien or mortgage on property that is created *by operation of law* without the parties express knowledge or agreement creating a *tacit mortgage* or *tacit maritime lien*.

15 A *tacit hypothecation* is a *hidden taking of assets* owned by a party other than the taker to be used as collateral for a loan without transferring the owner's title or use to the taker.

16 If the *owner of the assets* that the *taker takes* and uses as collateral for a loan retains the possession and use of the property, but the bank (*the lender to the taker/borrower*) can take and sell the property in the event that the borrower (*the taker of the assets*) defaults on the loan, the action is called, *in words of art,* a *pledge of assets* to the taker.

17 If the *taker of the assets* pledges the assets to a bank as collateral for a loan, the process is called, *in words of art,* a *re-hypothecation.*

18 In either a *hypothecation* or a *re-hypothecation* there is equitable risk to the actual owner of the assets.

19 Federal Reserve Notes are *"obligations of the United States"* to the American people and the Federal Reserve Bank. — *Federal Reserve Act, section 16; codified at 12 USC 411.*

20 *"The full faith and credit of the United States"* is the *substance taken from the American people by hypothecation,* the real property, wealth, assets and productivity of the people that has been *re-hypothecated* to the Federal Reserve Bank by the UNITED STATES for its obligation to the Federal Reserve and its issuance and backing of *borrowed Federal Reserve Notes* as legal tender *"for all taxes, customs, and other public dues".*

21 In other words, the *hidden taking of the assets* of the American people to be used in commerce by the UNITED STATES while leaving the people with possession and use of those assets is called, *in words of art,* an *hypothecation.*

22 If the taker of the assets (*the US*) pledges the same assets to a bank (*the FRB*) as collateral for a loan, the procedure is called, *in words of art,* a *re-hypothecation.*

23 In either a *hypothecation* or a *re-hypothecation* equitable *risk and interest accrues* to the owners of the assets

Money Doesn't Grow On Trees

(*the American people*), therefore *Federal Reserve Notes are* **priority obligations** *of the United States* **to the American people,** *and only* **secondary obligations** *of the United States* **to the Federal Reserve Bank.**

24 The commerce and credit of the people of the United States of America continues today under the *bankruptcy reorganization of the UNITED STATES, INC.,* as it has since 1933, *backed by the assets and wealth of the American people,* at risk for the federal government's obligations, currency and Federal Reserve Notes.

25 Under the 14th amendment, and numerous Supreme Court precedents, and in equity, the private property of the American people cannot be taken or pledged to the UNITED STATES for public use and put at risk without due process of law *and just compensation* (*remedial recovery of equity-interest via* **mutual offset credit exemption exchange**).

26 The UNITED STATES cannot pledge and risk the property and wealth of the people of America for any government purpose without legally providing them with REMEDY to recover the *equity-interest* that is due them on their *government-imposed risk.*

27 Courts have long ruled that to have one's property legally held as collateral or surety for a debt, even when one still owns it and has the use of it, is to DEPRIVE the owner of his property, since it is *at risk* and could be lost for the debt at any unknown time.

28 The United States Supreme Court said that the Constitution provides that *"private property shall not be taken for public use without just compensation."* (*United States v. Russell, 13 Wall, 623, 627*).

29 The *owners* of the assets are *presumed* to be *subro-*

gated to the *taker* and therefore liable for the taker's payments on his bank loan.

30 *Subrogation* is the substitution of one party for another whose debt the party pays, i.e., the sovereign is presumed to be substituted by the *ens legis* (government created) strawman.

31 *"The right of subrogation is not founded on contract. It is a creature of equity, enforced solely for the purpose of accomplishing the ends of substantial justice, and is independent of any contractual relations between the parties." —* Memphis & L.R.R.Co.v. Dow, 120 US 287, 302-302 (1887).

32 The *American people who own the assets and originating credit* are presumed to be subrogated to the *corporate UNITED STATES,* and are therefore liable for Congress' interest payments to the private non-federal, Federal Reserve on our *lawmaker's borrowed* and ever *increasing* National Debt.

33 Under the *laws of equity,* the United States of America cannot hypothecate and re-hypothecate the property and wealth of its private citizens, and put it at risk as collateral for its currency and credit, from the Federal Reserve Bank or any other bank, without legally providing its private citizens with an equitable **REMEDY** for recovery of what is due them and payable to them upon demand.

34 The United States government does not violate the law, nor the Constitution, by doing this, in order to collateralize its financial reorganization under bankruptcy obligation to the Federal Reserve Bank . . .

35 . . . because the United States government does in fact provide a legal **REMEDY** for the recovery of what is due to the people *as accrued interest* for risking their as-

sets and wealth so that it can legally hypothecate and re-hypothecate the private wealth and assets of the people who back its obligations and currency with their *substance and credit* and their implied consent.

36 The provisions for the **REMEDY** are found in "Public Policy" **HJR 192 of 1933** (a.k.a. Public Law 73-10) that *suspended* the gold standard for US currency, and *abrogated* the right to demand payment in gold, and made Federal Reserve Notes, for the first time, legal tender *"backed by the substance or credit of the nation"* — i.e., backed by the *substance and credit* of the people of America.

37 All US currency since 1933 is only **CREDIT** backed by the real property, wealth, assets, and future labor of the sovereign people of America, taken from the people *by presumptive pledge* by the UNITED STATES and *re-pledged* for a *secondary obligation* to the Federal Reserve Bank.

38 The sovereign American people cannot recover what is due them by anything drawn on Federal Reserve Notes of debt without expanding their risk and obligation to themselves, because any *recovery payments* backed by this type of currency (*negative FRNs*) would only increase the public debt that they are collateral for, which in equity would not satisfy anything, but which the **REMEDY** in equity is intended to reduce, because there is no longer any *actual money* of substance with which to pay anybody any ***thing***.

39 **There is no actual money in circulation today** by which debt owed by one party to another can actually be repaid.

40 Although declared "legal tender for all debts public and private" in the bankruptcy reorganization, Federal Reserve Notes of debt can only *discharge charges of debt,* whereas, debt must be "payed" with substance, i.e., gold,

silver, barter or some commodity, and extinguished.

41 For this reason the "Public Policy" of our current monetary system, **HJR 192 of 1933**, uses the technical term "discharge" as opposed to "payment" in laying out "Public Policy" for the monetary system of this *New World Order*, because a debt cannot pay a debt; a negative charge cannot neutralized a negative charge it just increases it. Minus $10 dollars, *minus* minus $10 dollars = minus $20 dollars.

42 Ever since 1933, commerce in the corporate UNITED STATES *and among its sub-corporate entities* has been conducted only with negative instruments of debt, i.e.debt note instruments by which the liability of a debt is "discharged" and transferred to someone else in a different form, but never *extinguished* until lawful, substance-backed *"money of account of the United States"* is restored.

43 The unpaid debt, created and expanded by the current Monetary plan, carries a "public liability" for its collection because when debt is discharged with debt instruments in commerce (*FRNs included*), the debt is **expanded** instead of being **extinguished,** thus *increasing* the public debt — a situation eventually fatal to any economy, as we are beginning to see happening today.

44 Congress and the government officials who devised the public laws and regulations that orchestrate the bankruptcy reorganization of the corporate UNITED STATES, anticipated the long term effect of the *debt based monetary system* that many in government feared, which we face today, in servicing the interest on trillions upon trillions of "dollars" of US negative corporate debt, so government officials made *statutory provisions* for **REMEDY** to provide *equity-interest recovery* and satisfaction to their *Sureties* (*the sovereign American people*), and at the same time *alleviate,*

if not *eliminate* the National Debt problem as well.

45 Since the real property, wealth and assets of all Americans is the *substance backing* the obligations, currency and credit of the UNITED STATES, such *credit* of the UNITED STATES is *tacitly offered,* and can therefore be used for *equity-interest recovery* via **mutual offset credit exemption exchange.**

46 The legal definitions written by Congress relating to legal tender provide for *private <u>un</u>incorporated persons* to issue **private promissory notes** for *equity-interest recovery* on their risk by the lawful-tender discharge of legitimate debts in commerce as **REMEDY** due them in the financial *reorganization in bankruptcy,* now in effect, and ongoing since 1933.

47 Public Policy **HJR 192 of 1933** provides for the discharge of every obligation "dollar for dollar" of and to the federal UNITED STATES, by discharging the obligations that *private <u>un</u>incorporated persons* owe against the same dollar for dollar amount of interest that the UNITED STATES owes to them, thus providing a **REMEDY** for orderly *equity-interest recovery,* and the eventual cancellation of the corporate public National Debt.

48 The public [national] debt is that portion of the total federal debt that is held by the public. (31 USC 1230).

49 Public Policy **HJR 192 of 1933** (Public Law 73-10) and 31 USC 5103 gives the *Secured Party Creditors of the UNITED STATES* the right to issue legal tender **promissory notes** *"upon the full faith and credit of the UNITED STATES"* as obligations of the federal UNITED STATES.

50 For these reasons, no creditor can require tender of any *specific type of currency* in place of **promissory notes** tendered in good faith "dollar for dollar" for legitimate debt.

51 The **REMEDY** for *equity-interest recovery* via ***mutual offset credit exemption exchange*** is codified in statutory law even though it is virtually unknown and seldom utilized in commerce today.

52 May the grace of our Lord Jesus Christ be with you all. Amen.

18
Watch What You Say

We are all God's children. We are not children of the State. We can discharge any debt in the public domain.

In the debt system we are working in, the most important tool we have is *a blue-ink pen.* With a *blue-ink pen* we can give credibility (credit) to any document that does not have *a blue-ink* signature on it.

Acceptance is a *banker acceptance.* You are accepting the document (the presentment) for payment. You are agreeing to pay it. When you pay the document — the negotiable instrument then belong to you.

A *blue-ink pen* is a very valuable tool in the world of commerce.

Anybody who sends you a bill who does not also send you a check with which to pay it, has created a public liability for which he didn't provide the remedy. Everything in commerce is a mirror image (the exact opposite) of real life when somebody sends you a presentment.

In the UCC (Uniform Commercial Code), in order to create a liability you have to make a presentment and present it to the libelee.

In court, the judge will say, to the defendant, *"Do you have a copy of the indictment?"* Meaning the information on which the indictment is based. Meaning the "charge" *against* you. When you say, *"No."* The judge will say, *"Well, here it is!"* And if you accept it, if you take it, then you accept the liability of the indictment and you have just *voluntarily* convicted yourself.

Or the judge might say, to the defendant, *"Do you understand the charge?"* If you reply that you understand the charge, you are saying that you "stand under" the charge, and that you are accepting the *liability* of the charge. And you have just *voluntarily* convicted yourself.

Some Redemptors used to get presentments from the IRS and the IRS would not send the check with which to pay it. So they would write back to the IRS and say, *"Thank you very much for what you sent me but you didn't send the check."*

After a time the IRS started sending the check. (Disguised as a *payment voucher*).

IRS presentments usually have a *coupon* attached at the bottom. That's the check. What you should do? Accept it for Value and return it to the sender (the IRS) to settle the debt. You don't have to have a coupon attached to do this.

When you accept and sign a document you turn it into currency in the same way a FRN (Federal Reserve Note) is currency. *Any piece of paper that is backed by the faith and confidence of the people can be turned into credit with which you can make exchanges of value with your credit.*

The purpose of *currency* is to enable the exchange (*the flow*) of commercial energy. The presentment has come to the fiction and you are accepting the presentment and satisfying the liability with your credit, for the fiction.

The signature on the promissory note creates the money stated on the promissory note that represents your commercial energy.

It's the *"full faith and credit of the People of the United States"* that gives FRNs the value that they have. Anybody on the street can do this. It is your signature (your credit sign) that creates the credit in your name.

In commerce, *the man is always exempt.* Accept the presentment, endorse it on the back, and send it to the IRS, because most of the commercial banks wouldn't know what to do with it.

A tax to you is already charged, but a bill is void of charges and has to be charged with your commercial energy before it can be used. In our system of commerce, the interest on any endeavor has to be returned to the creator — the Principal of the principle Account . . . hence the popular phrase: *"Return to Sender."*

A bill cannot be returned to the Principal because it has no charge to it. Commercial energy has to be in *existence* for a commercial charge to move it to ground. A copy of a presentment without a blue ink signature has no value. Charge it to the party that created the bill, via the IRS.

Once you charge the bill, the interest can be returned, via the Principal, to the the creator, to extinguish (zero out) the account.

GIVE YOURSELF CREDIT

19
You Have A Bond

We each have a bond, a trust fund set up for us upon our birth via our *"Registration of live Birth."* Somebody had to tell us what our name is. Our parents were already involved in the public domain. They wanted *"Little No Name"* to have access to the public benefits they enjoy that are provided by the public domain.

They had to give you a Title.

Your *"Application for live Berth"* assigned a place at the dock for you to "berth" your vessel in your Port of Entry — and a name and foot-print ("berth-mark") — forensic evidence of your arrival in the commercial public domain. A Title, such as JOHN, etc., creates a fiction in the Admiralty Venue. All vessels or dead people are titled in all caps names.

The One World Government has always been here. It has always existed from the beginning of the world.

They set up an account and gave it a reference number.

Your Birth Certificate Number is material evidence in the commercial domain that you exist. It is a prepaid credit exemption account. All participants in the public domain are pooled into an account that is accessed through the Social Security Number.

Any interchange for value between people is recorded in a trust that is automatically set-up — *a "foreign situs" trust.* The One World Government is the trustee of the trust and each individual person is a beneficiary of the trust.

A certain sum deemed the value of your lifework, say $1,000,000 dollars, is the commercial value of your credit in the commercial domain.

20
Your Supersedeas Bond

HJR 192 of June 5, 1933 is the bond the government uses to re-credit the people, *upon demand,* because the Roosevelt administration took away the people's gold.

HJR 192 is an insurance policy that cancels the execution of debt required by law with the favor of Grace. It allows the "Angel of Debt" to pass over us for our commercial Redemption.

The bond is on the debt side of the ledger of the corporate United States. The bond is the Grace that created our EXEMPTION from any liability to pay our debts. This is our saving Grace. Under Grace, the law falls away to create a more perfect union contract.

Public Policy removes our liability to pay our debts by making all contracts null and void that require payment in substance or more debt (federal reserve notes) because there is no substance money to make payment with.

A debt has to only to be discharged.

The word "pay" is equated with silver and gold or some *thing* of substance like a first-born lamb which requires an *execution of work* to remove the liability for the *execution* of debt that must otherwise take place.

The word "discharge" is equated with credits and debits of commercial paper.

You cannot pay a bill with a bill. You cannot pay a debt with a debt. You need a bond to pay a bill and that's what Public Policy does. Public Policy is the bond that pays our debts. It is a promise to pay all charges that we accept for payment.

If a debt exists, the best we can do is to write it off, but that can only be done if we return the bill to its maker via the IRS as our **mutual offset credit exemption exchange**.

Corporations discharge *debt instruments,* but people can pay with *asset instruments* instead.

Bail notices (security required for a release) state, *"Pay by check or money order, do not send cash."*

HJR 192 makes it against Public Policy to pay a debt with debt instruments, which is what cash is, therefore one's order for credit (one's bill) needs to be accepted and returned to the presenter directly or via the IRS.

HJR 192 removes the debtor's obligation to pay a debt, making in against Public Policy to pay a debt with a debt. FRNs are instrument of debt.

We only have to discharge the debt "dollar for dollar" with our credit (the only credit that there is) by *exchanging the "bill for the bond"* — the bond that represents our **credit exemption** — exchanging a "past liability" for a "future liability" by "passingover" the "present liability" of the note.

There is no money with which to credit an account. Our **commercial energy** is the credit that the industrial society — the public — needs, to adjust their ledgers. They need our **endorsement** as evidence of our having discharged the charge, for them to be able to close the account, otherwise they have an aging accounts-receivable that they cannot close without our endorsement, our **acknowledgment** that public benefits were provided and received in the private domain.

As the operator of the account, they need to charge us with their commercial energy so we can charge the commercial energy back to them and therefore ground the account by *exchanging* the energy (the tax) back to the presenter directly or via the IRS.

Debt must be discharged "dollar-for-dollar" just as sin must be repented of once it occurs. As soon as we realize that sin has occurred we must acknowledge and be forgiven for that sin, or we stand in default.

The moment that a debt exists it must be written off to balance the account. We have to "accept the charge" to allow the maker to close the account through our name.

Maxim: **My name is my bond.**

In other words, my *signature* represents my bond.

Our acceptance and endorsement zeros the account by grounding the charge back to whence it came and closes its delinquently held, open account.

We can't write off the debt without charging it back to the origin from whence it came (dust to dust) because we do not hold the deficient account. Our fiduciary agent (the presenter) holds the account so we must provide him with a tax return by sending him *the credit of our acceptance* directly to him, or via the IRS, so he can write off our liability via *HIS internal revenue service,* the bookkeeper of his firm.

We do not need to make a payment that is acceptable to the claimant. We "Accept for Value" the credit and return it to the presenter via the IRS. We endorse and return his offer to the strawman, to the IRS.

The document is the collateral itself, not what the paper represents. The property goes with the paper but it cannot be used as a method of payment under Public Policy which is Grace.

Many people think that when our money was taken away

from society that the people became slaves to *the* **New World Order** *of the* **One World Government**, but this is not true, unless they *voluntarily* choose for it to be so. The people were *freed,* instead. We were freed from every obligation that the public society could create. We were freed from any obligation that we could incur because we cannot "pay" a debt with a debt. There is no money with which to "pay."

Public Policy is the **Supersedeas Bond**, the bond that *supersedes* all other bonds, because it *by-passes* — or "passes over" — our *inability to pay.*

Public Policy is the more perfect contract because it operates on Grace to pay our debts, after we have done all that we could do. We do as much as we can, then Mercy and Grace kick in, being our EXEMPTION that makes the payment *for us* so long as we *accept full responsibility for the charge . . .* so long as we *accept the redemption offered by Christ.*

"By so much was Jesus made a surety of a better testament." — Hebrews 7:22.

"And I saw a new heaven and a new earth : for the first heaven and the first earth were passed away ; and there was no more sea." — Revelation 21: 1.

21
Your Mirror-Image Strawman

As a child, you have had an imaginary friend. You may be surprised to learn that evidence exists that you have had a make-believe twin from the time your mother and father permitted a Birth Certificate to be applied for in your name. This make-believe friend is not real, but artificial. It is a strawman, an artificial entity that has a name very similar to yours. Here is a definition of "strawman."

> "A 'front'; a third party who is put up in name only to take part in a transaction. Nominal party to a transaction..." — Black's Law Dictionary, 6th Edition.

> "The term is also used in commercial and property contexts when a transfer is made to a party, the strawman, simply for the purpose of **retransmitting** to the transferer in order to accomplish some purpose not otherwise permitted." — Barron's, 3rd Edition.

So, in layman's terms what is a strawman?

The strawman is an artificial person created by law shortly after you were born, via the registration of the application for your birth certificate. The name for the strawman is your name in ALL CAPITAL LETTERS.

The inscription on your birth certificate is also your name in all-capital letters. The English language has precise rules of grammar that make no provision for writing proper nouns in all-capital letters. So your name spelled with all-capital letters is a fictitious name.

Your strawman has a "same-sounding-name" as your name but it names an artificial entity which exists only "by force of, or in contemplation of law."

The all-caps name is not your "true name" which consists of your <u>given name</u> (<u>or Christian name</u>) plus the <u>surname</u> (<u>your family name</u>) and it appears in scrip with only initial letters capitalized. The all-caps version of your name is a TRADENAME, the name under which you "do business" in commerce.

We may also say that the strawman is a *"person"* according to the legal dictionary.

> *"Person. 1. a human being. 2. An entity (such as a corporation) that is recognized by law as having the rights and duties of a human being…"* — Blacks Law Dictionary, 7th Edition.

The strawman may *also* be said to be an *"artificial person"* which is defined in the legal dictionary.

> *"An entity, such as a corporation, created by law and given certain legal rights and duties of a human being; a being, real or imaginary, who for the purpose of legal reasoning is treated more or less as a human being. – Also termed fictitious person; juristic person; legal person; moral person."* — Blacks Law Dictionary, 7th Edition.

A strawman may *also* be thought of as a *"legal fiction."*

"Legal fiction. Assumption of fact made by court as basis for deciding a legal question. A situation contrived by the law to permit a court to dispose of a matter ..." — Black's Law Dictionary 5th Edition.

As we explore further, we must distinguish between the *strawman* (an "it" or "person") and the real, flesh and blood *human being* which we will call a "man".
Man has a legal definition.

"human being. A person of the male sex. A male of the human species above the age of puberty. In the most extended sense the term includes not only the adult male sex of the human species, but women and children. ... In feudal law, a vassal; a tenant or feudatory." — Blacks Law Dictionary, 5th Edition.

So we conclude that "man" is a term of nature. But who created nature? Some would say "God," others would say the "Creator" (a term often used by the Founders of our country), while others might hold a different view. On the other hand, we see "person" as a term of civil law. Who is the creator of civil law?

"Civil law ... a rule of civil conduct prescribed by the supreme power of a state ... the civil or municipal law of the Roman empire." — Ballentine's Law Dictionary, 3rd Edition.

So kings, emperors or legislative bodies acting in a sovereign capacity are the so-called "creators" of civil law. When our government acts as a sovereign it is acting *outside* of its constitutional authority.

So we see that a man and a person are very *different* terms identifying very *different* things.

If you study Roman civil law, you will see that it originates and uses fictions of law — concepts that are *contrary* to the natural order of things and based upon *presumptions* that are not true. This "person" recognized in the civil law is a fictional entity. The strawman is a "person," a *public name* that is recognized in civil society.

We've mentioned "legal fiction" and "fiction of law" so let's see how these are defined.

> *"Fiction of law. An assumption or supposition of law that something which is or may be* false *is true, or that a state of facts exists which has never* really *taken place. An* assumption, *for purposes of justice, of a fact that does not or may not exist. A rule of law which* assumes *as true, and will not allow to be disproved, something which is* false, *but not impossible." — Black's Law Dictionary 5th Edition.*

This distinction between a man and a person is a difficult concept to grasp. But a proper understanding of the *relationship* between the government, the man, and the strawman is essential to gaining increased freedom. While the concept of these relationships is very simple, there are some foundational principles that must be explored.

We have mentioned that the strawman is an artificial entity or person. But there are several *types* of organizations, or artificial entities. There are *corporation soles, aggregate corporations, municipal corporations, revocable living trusts (sole),* and *unincorporated business organizations.*

Many people use these entities for various reasons including maintaining personal control over their assets, protection from lawsuits and judgments, avoidance of probate, avoidance of estate taxes, reduction in tax liability, and many other reasons.

We will look into the difference between a **sole entity** and an **aggregate entity;** the construction of these entities and the results of that construction as they apply to the strawman.

In all organizations there are *two* **basic operational positions***:* 1) The chief executive officer/president/chairman/trustee (the **governing** position); and 2) The stock holder/owner/beneficiary (the **beneficiary** position).

A *sole corporation,* as defined by Black's Law Dictionary, is one consisting of *one person only,* and his *successors* in some particular station, who are incorporated by law in order to give them some legal *capacities and advantages,* particularly that of *perpetuity,* which in their natural state as persons they could not have.

In a corporation sole, one person holds *both operational positions* of the organization.

A corporation sole may be established under legislative authority. It is considered by statute to be a *"citizen"* of the government. As such, the safe-guards of the Bill of Rights do not extend to the *corporate sole.* The courts have warned that statutory licensed *sole proprietorships* are in fact a *government agency* by definition of how they are created. Most people who choose to be a *sole organization* do so because they maintain personal control over their assets.

An aggregate corporation such as a corporation or business trust, according to Black's Law Dictionary, is composed of a number of individuals vested with limited liability corporate powers.

With an aggregate organization, different parties must hold the *governing* and *beneficiary* positions. If the *same* party holds them, they are a *corporate sole.*

Family members are always counted as *one party,* therefore it would be a *corporate sole* organization. In an *aggregate* organization, the one who benefits is *immune* from damage claims or the liabilities of the governors. In an *aggregate* corporation, the *governors* control the assets for the *beneficiaries.* In other words, the *beneficiaries surrender* control of the assets over to someone else.

The founder of the wealthy Rockefeller family once said that one his secrets to wealth was to *"own nothing, but control everything".*

In other words, always function from an *aggregate relationship* as the *beneficiary.* Do not *own* the strawman; *control* the strawman. If you are not the owner of the strawman *you are not liable for his debts or obligations.*

If you are in *control* you have the highest *lien hold interest* on the strawman and *you* must be paid before anyone else collects from the strawman, and you *cannot* go to jail or prison for his wrongdoing.

A look at the structure of the strawman entity shows the ownership/control relationship and which position it is best to hold.

Commercial redemption is a term used among freedom loving people to describe the process of regaining control of one's strawman. Prior to the *Commercial Process of Redemption* (CPR) the man was considered both a *beneficiary* and *surety* for the strawman.

After commercial redemption, the man is seen to be a *beneficiary,* but no longer the *surety* for the strawman. After commercial redemption the man is the *controller* and *creditor* holding the highest *lien hold interest* in the strawman. The man is now in an *aggregate* relationship with the strawman. He does not *own the strawman* but he *benefits from* and *controls the strawman* by his primary lien hold interest.

In this country, power was granted to the government by the people, *individually,* to create the states, and by the people, *as a whole,* to create the national government.

Once the people decided, *individually,* to create the State, they can only change the policy or laws of the State as people *collectively,* because they have agreed to become part of the *public.* They are but one person in a larger body of people that act *collectively.* The people are in both the state government and national government at that same time (*dual citizenship*). The public government is an artificial entity. The government is owned and controlled by the same people, so the government is a **sole organization** not an **aggregate organization**. As long as a man is dealing *publicly,* he is in a *sole relationship* with the public. The strawman, *being artificial,* lives in the artificial "Wizard-of-Oz-place" called *the public.*

At the same time that people are acting **collectively** in the larger body of people called the State and national government, they maintain their ability to act **individually** on a **private** basis.

The people did not give up any of the rights that they **did not** delegate to the government — they *retained those rights.* A man can *contract privately* as he sees fit. The government cannot interfere with the *private contracts* of men.

Money Doesn't Grow On Trees

The *strawman* lives in the *public side* of government. He is part of the *public government* and functions under the laws of the public, not the re-public.

This is necessary and proper because *the creator of an entity has the right to govern it.* Since the government created the strawman, it is only right that the strawman lives under the rules of it's creator, the government.

But once the strawman has been *commercially redeemed,* the government is no longer in control of the strawman. The strawman is *now controlled* by the man using his *private right to make contracts.* The man has left the *public* as a *surety* in sole relationship to the strawman, to live *privately* as *creditor/beneficiary* in an *aggregate relationship* with the strawman.

As far as this *relationship* is concerned, the strawman is *privately controlled.* The strawman still exists as a *public entity* because that is the only world in which he has *reality.* His relationship with the *man* is *private.* The relationship with *the living being man* is *a controlling* relationship because the man has a *higher priority lien* on the strawman than the government has.

Now that we understand who the strawman is, it is appropriate to ask, *"Who benefits from the creation of the strawman?"*

The strawman benefits the *creator* (the government), *any corporation* that uses *it and you* to its advantage.

The government began benefiting from the strawman when the UNITED STATES, INC. went bankrupt in 1933. When this happened, the governors of all the States met to discuss what they should do. The state governors "pledged" to fund the bankruptcy. They pledged the **assets** and **commercial energy** of the people in the states, to the federal government. They promised to back the federal "government" and secure the federal (national) debt.

But there was one problem: The governors of the States could only speak for the people *in their public capacity.* They could not pledge *private living human beings* and *their private property.* So it was necessary to create a "bridge" between the *living people* and the *creditors of the bankruptcy.* The answer was to create *strawmen (public utilities)* to stand in the place of the people. *Then* the only problem rested in devising a scheme whereby the people could be induced to *voluntarily agree to contract with the strawman as its surety.*

When the governors made the pledge, they agreed to register the **application form** for the birth certificates of the people with the U.S. Department of Commerce. The application form for the birth certificate is the **security instrument** used as collateral to back the pledge.

The strawman, *the legal fiction,* was created by using the name on the birth certificate and writing it in all capital letters, the designation for a *legal fiction* or the name of a *vessel, ship* or *boat.* Then *because of the "pledge"* the people were *devised* to be the **accommodation party, representative** and **surety** for the legal fiction.

This is how they made us responsible to pay back the National Debt, the debt of the bankrupt UNITED STATES.

When the "government" or any *corporation* uses any process whatsoever, they are using it *against the legal fiction* which they want the people to think is themselves.

But when a name is written in all capital letters it is not the name of a real person. It is the designation of **a legal fiction,** an entirely separate entity. A living human being cannot be a legal fiction and a legal fiction cannot be a living human being. One is *real or natural* and the other is *an ens legis creation of "law."*

Because the entire thing is based on paying off the bankruptcy of the United States, the strawman is the **debtor** and the "government" is the **agent for the creditors** who are the international bankers who own the Federal Reserve.

You must realize that the debt is not *your* debt *personally.* It is *your strawman's* debt. You have been functioning as a voluntary representative for a ***cestui que trust account*** (***your strawman***) *by discharging your strawman's bills with fiat money instead of paying them with your* **mutual offset credit exemption exchange.**

When you established your first checking account, you unknowingly accepted this relationship with the trust that the government established in your name. You have not had control of this trust because you have never claimed it and your parents could not control it for you because they were wards of the state, like you.

The System maintains the illusion by artifice and deceptive design.

Look at your checkbook. Your name is an ALL CAPS named BUSINESS CORPORATION that the bank presumes you to be.

A clue to that presumption is in the line on your checks over which you sign your name. The ***MicroPrint signature line.*** (MP) It's not a line. It's printed words, some of the finest printing you will ever encounter. It says something like:
AUTHORIZED REPRESENTATIVE AUTHORIZED REPRESENTATIVE AUTHORIZED REPRESENTATIVE AUTHORIZED REPRESENTATIVE (etc., etc.)

In the corporate world, only the ***authorized representative*** of a CORPORATION has the authority to sign ***the corporation's checks.*** So you, *the human being,* have been given the *authority* to sign the checks of ***your money trust*** (***your strawman***) — ***an incorporated fiction.***

22
Promissory Notes Are Legal Tender

HJR 192 of June 5, 1933 made Federal Reserve Notes (FRNs) legal tender for all public and private debts.

In a letter from the Federal Reserve Bank of Cleveland, Associate General Counsel, Oliver Ireland, said in confirmation of HJR 192:

> "To the extent that Federal Reserve Notes (FRNs) represent an obligation of liability, they represent the claim of the holder thereof against the United States government. Therefore, a person holding or using FRNs as payment does not become liable for the claim against the United States government, but rather becomes the Holder of such a claim, the Person entitled to enforce the claim against the United States government."

HJR 192 of 1933 declares that the debts of the United States are dischargeable by FRNs which are legal tender as a matter of law. (31 USC 5103).

> Section 5103. Legal Tender
> United States coins and currency (including Federal reserve notes and circulating notes of Federal reserve banks and national banks) are legal tender for all debts, public charges, taxes, and dues. Foreign gold or silver coins are not legal tender for debts.

In the same letter Associate General Counsel, Oliver Ireland, addressed the issue of redemption of FRNs for gold and silver coin stating:

> *"We were previously aware that FRNs cannot be redeemed for gold or silver coinage, yet the fact remains that FRNs, even though they are 'legal tender', should always be <u>redeemable for lawful money</u> because <u>notes are a promise to pay money</u>. This fact is supported by the current wording of 12 USC 411 which state that FRNs '<u>shall be redeemed in lawful money on demand...</u>' which undeniably means their respective faces according to the Federal Reserve Act of 1913, until later legislation eliminated gold and then silver redemption."*

According to law, Federal Reserve Notes and circulating notes of Federal Reserve Banks are legal tender exchangeable for other Federal Reserve Notes **and circulating notes of Federal Reserve Banks.**

Since promissory notes are legal tender used by banks every day, promissory notes are legal tender for everyone to use for the payment of public and private debts.

Promissory notes represent the right of the Holder to enforce the note's promise against the government of the United States.

23
We The People Provide The Credit

"No state shall...make any <u>thing</u> but gold and silver coin a tender in payment of debts..." — <u>Art. 1, Sec. 10, clause 1</u> of the Constitution <u>FOR</u> the United States of America and the CONSTITUTION <u>OF</u> THE UNITED STATES, INC.

In order to circumvent this constitutional rule and in order to make paper Federal Reserve Notes (FRNs) *"a tender in payment of debts"* Congress turned to its *"power...to borrow money on the credit (of the people) of the United States."* — <u>Art. 1, Sec. 10, clause 1</u>.

Since Congress borrows "money substitutes" (FRNS) on the basis of **my credit** since I am one of the people of the United States, Congress gives **me** an unlimited **credit exemption** that I can use to discharge the debts that I cannot **"pay"** with FRNs because FRNs are not **real** *"money of account of the United States"* that **"pays"** debts. Congress permits me to use my *personal credit exemption* to **"pay"** charges that FRNs can only **"discharge."**

Part four of the 1040 ES instruction booklet under "Estimated Tax Worksheet" in reference to "exemptions" says: *"If you can be claimed as a dependent on another person's return your personal exemption is <u>not</u> allowed."*

This says in effect that **my** personal exemption **is allowed** when and if I am not claimed as a dependent on another *"persons"* (*corporation's*) return. In other words, the

Money Doesn't Grow On Trees

industrial society will claim my *personal exemption — my mutual offset credit exemption exchange* — if I don't claim it for myself.

The above declaration is a second witness to my **REMEDY** for being an accommodating party to the corporate UNITED STATES via my pledge of credit to the public debt. I am claiming the UNITED STATES as my dependant because I am *accommodating* the UNITED STATES with my pledge of personal credit to the public debt.

We the People are the source of the *commercial energy* that our credit represents.

We the people provide the credit for every instrument that we endorse the very instant we endorsed it.

Our signature represents the intangible personal credit that we provide. We only have to pay for what we get with money substitutes (FRNs) because our suppliers usurp *our personal credit exemption* for their own use when we fail to object and do not demand *our personal credit exemption* for ourselves. *They can't do this when we object.*

All taxes are interest payments that accrue from the principle of the *lenders of personal credit* (*meaning us*) to the lending institutions of the corporate UNITED STATES, and these interest payments must be returned *to the lenders of personal credit* (*to us*), *when so claimed,* for the close of escrow lest we be found guilty *"for failing to make a return."*

My credit exemption is assured; it is my supersedeas bond because:

"No state shall...make any...law impairing the obligation of contracts." — Art. 1, Sec. 10, clause 1, US Constitution.

24
The Truth Now Told

The United States and its subdivisions (which municipalities are) has been operating in a Chapter-11, bankruptcy reorganization since 1933, and since there was not enough gold, and silver ("money of account of the United States") to back the nation's currency, pay, its debts, and enable the businesses of the country to pay theirs, Congress passed laws that replaced the *substance money* needed to pay debts with the unredeemable, paper promissory notes of the Federal Reserve Bank.

Ordinarily this would have been a gross violation of the US Constitution that requires our currency to be backed by gold and silver coins, but it is *not* a violation of the Constitution *in a bankruptcy reorganization* which is a temporary suspension of normal obligations by law; for the protection of the debtor (the corporate UNITED STATES) from its creditors (we the people of the United States).

When Treasury notes come due they are not paid, but are refinanced by new T-Bills to back the currency and cover the debts.

You can't do that with debt that you owe unless you are protected from creditors in a bankruptcy reorganization that is regularly and constantly being restructured to keep the organization alive.

Congress legislated that the new money shall be backed by **"the credit of the United States"** and represent ***"a mortgage on all the...property of the people in the nation."***

So who holds the mortgage?

Under the Constitution and laws of equity the United States could not borrow or pledge the property and wealth of its *private citizens* and put them at risk as collateral backing the nation's currency and credit, *except in bankruptcy reorganization* where the *private citizens* become the Principals and Prime Creditors of the United States and its subsidiaries holding a REMEDY for the recovery of interest due them *on their loan of credit to the public domain* — and this is exactly what we have in HJR 192 of 1933.

As prime-creditors outside of the bankruptcy (the citizens of the United States) could not recover what was due them via federal Reserve Notes (FRNs) *without increasing the debt* since there was no longer any *actual "money of account of the United States"* (gold and silver coin) with which to pay tangible value (substance) for anything.

Here were the America people at the heart of the depression in 1933 whose real property and wealth were collateralizing the government's currency and debt having no way to pay their debts with lawful *"money of account of the United States."*

So HJR 192 of 1933 resolved that **"a right to require payment in...a particular kind of coin or currency...is against Public Policy."** This resolution allowed the people who backed the *bankruptcy reorganization* of the United States with their credit (*we the people*) to recover their equity by *discharging debts they owed to subcorporate entities of the United States,* by the **adjustment and set-off of mutual exchanges** against a "dollar for dollar" amount of the United States debt and its sub-corporate entities, owed back to them through drafts, bills of exchange and promissory notes tendered for that purpose.

An arcane system almost like barter is still in effect today for those who discover and access it.

Accordingly, the definition of legal tender still includes **"circulating notes...of national banks"** which have not been legal as currency for almost eighty years...but the definition maintained still includes **the holders of U.S. Corporate** bankruptcy *reorganizational **debt*** who collectively and nationally **constitute,** by statutory definition, **a "national banking association"** or "national bank," since 1933, **having the right to issue credit instruments to recover interest due them on the public debt.**

The government doesn't publicize this for obvious reasons and they make it difficult to determine how to do this. *But for those who succeed, the government will not dishonor a Prime Creditor's presentment for remedial recovery via the REMEDY provided.*

The entire bankruptcy reorganization continues in equity with our implied consent backed by the credit of our assets and wealth — still at risk as collateral for the currency and national debt of the UNITED STATES and its sub-corporate entities — because the REMEDY to recover what is due us as citizens is there . . . even though we are not told that it exists, *nor how to access it.*

If the government were to ever dishonor the REMEDY, it would be a debtor seeking to operate outside of his bankruptcy reorganization plan, on the sly, without clean hands which is a criminal offense, for those responsible could eventually cause the entire government debt to we the people, the holders and creditors of it, to be called due by us.

This is another reason the government is afraid to be on record about our supersedeas bond lest someone says the wrong thing and brings disaster. This is too sensitive and volatile a subject to take lightly.

The individual creditor or sub-corporate entity operating within the bankruptcy who dishonors a holder's recovery of what is due him in discharge of public debt places himself outside of the bankruptcy's protection from its creditors in equity, and he is then open to **involuntary bankruptcy** and liquidation of his assets to the amount of the debt the principal creditor had sought to discharge, and to the full amount of that sub-corporate entity's share of the public debt owed to the prime creditors and holders of it, if he chooses to pursue it.

Notarial Protest and Dishonor are *non-court administrative proceedings* for the common citizen to initiate in a private capacity if necessary.

Every time the Federal Debt ceiling is raised by Congress they are restructuring the bankruptcy reorganization of the government's debt so that we all can continue in commerce.

The US Corporate public debt is trillions and trillions of dollars. The whole system is like a house of cards teetering in the wind and there are powerful unseen forces working at whatever cost to keep peace and good relations with the Principals and Secured Parties who provide the collateral for the country's currency, commerce and credit and who hold the first mortgage on the nation to keep all that we have going. *Therefore the processing of these instruments is a very sensitive delicate confidential private matter.*

The United States government doesn't want to have to openly recognize all this, but when put in a position of legally having to acknowledge or deny it those responsible *will not deny it.* To refuse a standing obligation of the United

States would be a criminal act for them. But more, it would place the United States government operating outside its bankruptcy reorganization in violation of the law, and would collapse the entire financial system built on credit reorganization.

Be discrete about sharing this information with others. These concepts are not for the untaught public.

But the Secretary of the Treasury and those in charge cannot pay the debt either for there is no money. To do so would be public testimony, official witness and admission by the government to the fact that the REMEDY exists.

Millions of people would start discharging their debts against the REMEDY. The result would be chaos!

Due to the sensitive nature of this constructive trust — created as a REMEDY for the Secured Party Creditors of the U.S. Corporate's reorganization debt — the government will not ever be able to pay it.

But they really don't have to.

As long as the government does not refuse, deny, return, or dishonor our discharge claims, they have accepted them and whether paid or not in law, they have permitted our claims of discharge *to become legally enforceable obligations of the United States* and the parties and banks involved can legally gain relief through the United States' regulatory avenues to obtain more credit, or release credit due customer's account.

It is not testimony or acknowledgment by the government of the **REMEDY** because their silence does not indicate why they have remained silent.

Nevertheless, the government has provided practical means for recovery to we the people, the prime Creditor and Holders of the National Debt.

It is not likely that any agency or division of government under the direct or indirect control of the Secretary of the Treasury has dishonored by refusing to accept the instruments for which the United States is legally liable.

Fascinating isn't it?

The evidence of what is happening is all around us in the news every day. It is very impressive. And it is best for us not to bring it up.

Only show that you know it.

Just let it be *known* that you know.

"Ye shall know the truth, and the truth shall set you free." — Jesus the Christ at John 8:32.

25
Remedy Review

Affidavit of Information

The biological property of every American has been preregistered as a "corporation-of-one" in a national system of Public Policy designed to keep track of and control the people, at peace, under the ancient System of Pledge.

Every American has been preregistered as a 14th Amendment corporate citizen of the corporate United States as the source of "credit" supporting the promissory notes of the private non-federal Federal Reserve, that we mistakenly call "dollars."

The United States holds a security interest in each United States "corporation-of-one" by the operation of the Law Merchant under a scheme of secured transactions according to commercial contract law under the Uniform Commercial Code commonly called the UCC.

Since 1933 you and your credit and the credit of all other Americans have been pledged as collateral for the debt of the corporate UNITED STATES without your knowledge or consent. This is unlawful conversion, but legal and in force until we take back our "implied consent" by the special lawful and legal *Commercial Process of Redemption* (CPR).

We have unknowingly been registered to be collateral for a mortgage held by *foreign financiers,* from the founding of this Nation, in 1776.

"The answer to the conditions we face today is 1776."

Perhaps you assume that the name on the tax statement that you have received at some point in time, or on your drivers license, or telephone and power bill, is yours, and so you respond to these *commercial presentments* as though the name were yours. This is involuntary servitude.

To make this involuntary servitude legal the government provides us with a REMEDY.

It doesn't matter that the REMEDY is hidden by legalese that makes it difficult to access and apply.

That the REMEDY is not widely in use today presumes our knowledge of it, and our choice to not use it, for "ignorance of the law is no excuse."

The REMEDY is *not impossible* to apply just seemingly difficult . . . and *implausible to perceive.*

Your status as a subject of the state is based upon the PRESUMPTION *that if you did not wish to be so encumbered to the State,* you would use the Law to do something about it. As long as you *do not take advantage of the REMEDY that the law provides,* the State PRESUMES that you are content to remain in servitude to the state and be used as collateral for the federal National Debt.

Can such a premise be true?

It seems totally out of step with everything we have ever known about our world, our nation, our government, and our relationship to the State, but it is so.

Under HJR 192 passed by Congress 77 years ago, on June 5, 1933, it is public policy NOT to pay debts — as unbelievable as this might seem.

It is impossible to pay debts because there is no "money of account of the United States" with which to pay them.

No one can compel anyone to pay a debt with silver or gold or any specific monetary instrument of his demand.

Once a debt is created one's *liability to pay* can only be discharged by tendering it to someone else, *or back upon its creator to cancel the charge.*

With the advent of the bankruptcy of the corporate United States in 1933 all debts can be discharged by one's promise to pay, when legitimate "money of account of the United States" is restored to use, or by one's MOCEE.

A presentment is an offer, or bid, put forward for "payment" or "acceptance and discharge." **Refusing an offer creates a *controversy* that puts the refuser in default, making him liable for the presentment value himself,** instead of being the maker or accepter of the offer.

There can be no ***controversy*** in bankruptcy for in bankruptcy *all debts are discharge.*

"The judicial power shall extend to all cases, in law and equity, arising under this Constitution, to controversies ..." — *Article III, Sect. 2, clause 1, US Constitution.*

With no ***controversies*** allowed in bankruptcy, the judicial jurisdiction may be called into play when a ***judiciable controversy*** is created by someone refusing to accept an offer. You must either "pay" or "discharge."

Once you "accept the debt for its value" and "return it for value" to its source directly or via the IRS, the debt is discharged according to public insurance policy **HJR 192 of 1933**, and when *you have returned your acceptance to the sender,* he must credit you on his ledger with having discharged the charge.

Public Policy is the maritime security insurance bond that

settles the debts of the Redemptor's state-created vessel-strawman.

A verbal or written security agreement with the state-created vessel-strawman is the basis of the security contract.

You can register your private security bond in the public domain as the basis of your ***mutual off-set credit exemption exchange,*** if you wish but it is not required.

You are exempt from paying because you are the principle security ***"holder-in-due-course"*** (controller) of your strawman in the public domain.

You are THE "first-in-line" and "first-in-time" ***secured party creditor*** (SPC) of any commercial transaction that you endorse with your credit-sign, your blue ink signature.

HJR 192 of 1933 states that the people of the United States can use *any kind of currency, coin, or personal promissory note* to discharge public and private debt as long as it is used in the normal course of business in the United States.

At first gold and silver and United States Notes backed by gold and silver were used as currency to pay debts, but later the Federal Reserve and the corporate UNITED STATES provided a new medium of exchange — ***promissory notes*** that are available for us to use to discharge public and private debt today via MERCY/MOCEE — ***mutual offset credit exemption exchange.***

26
It's Only A Game

All systems of belief are a series of events characterized first by the birth of a good idea. This idea gradually develops into dogma architectured by other humans, and finally ends up carved into the rock of *"our-rules-you-must-adhere-to-or-else,"* by still more humans.

The original concept came from a human just like you and me. He simply had a revolutionary idea about how the world could work and shared his idea with other people. Those people then took his idea and ran with it and eventually developed it into the "Rules Carved into Rock" because most people aren't convinced of the great value of their own ideas. They cling to the same rock others are grasping for, the Rock of absolute Truth.'

Absolutes make people feel safe. Absolutes, *to the believer,* can't be argued with, challenged or changed. Wars are fought over which absolute Truth is the correct one. The debate over *which text is correct* has been the number-one cause of violent death in the *long-time* favorite game of

I AM RIGHT! and YOU ARE WRONG!

If it's only a game then we all have a part to play. The author's part is to be a **potentiator of the mind** to remind you that "it's only a game."

For instance, a certain game-player once told this story about "Monopoly".

While visiting with friends, he was invited to play the game but he declined.

His highly competitive host began to taunt him about his abilities, *and what-not.* After a few minutes of taunting, he replied, "All right, I'll join your game, but you won't like how I play."

With that, they set up the game for four players.

After a time — all players having accumulated property to one degree or other — our hero unfortunately landed on one of his host's expensive squares and became liable for a heavy tax. The host smiled with cunning, satisfaction and glee and put out his hand to receive the monopoly money.

"We can play this hand in two ways," says the man, "you can let me go on and we'll forget about the tax, or you can *take* the money from me, in which case I will give all of my properties to Bob over here, and he will undoubtedly win the game."

"You can't do that," said the host, "It's against the rules."

"I'll tell you what," our hero replied, "if you can find the rule that says I can't do it, I'll hand over the tax and we'll continue the game."

Of course, the host dug out the rule book and pored through it like a mad-man possessed, but — sure enough — there was no rule for or against our hero's tactic.

Realizing he was beaten, and not being prepared to let anyone else win by default, the host reliquished his right to take the tax and they played on.

Every time our man landed on another's property, he made the same offer and each player let him pass untaxed. He eventually won by a long margin, and laughed as he reminded them, "I said you wouldn't like how I play."

By deferring to rules that others have set, and by following those rules to the letter, because it seems *safer to do so,* we risk being bound and hampered by those very rules.

The key is trusting your own ability to fly by the seat of your pants (intuition) when you realize that you have the ability to level the playing field by exercising your mind instead of automatically deferring to others in the game.

A fundamental part of enjoying the game is knowing what the rules are, and what they are not — while never compromising the integrity of the game — and *whom-so-ever* wins:

In the end it is You.

27
Recall Notice

[**This timely message was sent in by an anonymous donor**].

The Maker of all human beings (**the Creator, GOD**) is recalling all units manufactured, regardless of make or year, due to a serious defect in the primary and central component of the heart.

This is due to a malfunction in the original prototype units, code-named Adam and Eve, resulting in the reproduction of the same defect in all subsequent units. This defect has been technically termed "**Sub-sequential Internal Non-morality,**" more commonly known as **SIN.**, as it is primarily expressed.

Some of the symptoms include:

1. *Loss of direction*
2. *Foul vocal emissions*
3. *Amnesia of origin*
4. *Lack of peace and joy*
5. *Selfish or violent behavior*
6. *Depression or confusion in the mental component*
7. *Fearfulness*
8. *Idolatry*
9. *Rebellion*

The Manufacturer, who is neither liable nor at fault for this defect, is providing factory-authorized repair and service free of charge to correct this defect.

The Repair Technician, JESUS, has most generously offered to bear the entire burden of the staggering cost of these repairs. There is no additional fee required.

The number to call for repair in all areas is P-R-A-Y-E-R. Once connected, please upload your burden of SIN through the REPENTANCE procedure. Next, download ATONEMENT from the Repair Technician, JESUS, into the heart component.

No matter how big or small the SIN defect is, JESUS will replace it with:

1. *Love*
2. *Joy*
3. *Peace*
4. *Patience*
5. *Gentleness*
6. *Goodness*
7. *Faith*
8. *Meekness*
9. *Self-control*

Please see the operating Manual, the BIBLE, for further details on the implementation of these repairs.

WARNING: Continuing to operate the human being unit *without correction* voids any manufacturer warranties, exposing the unit to dangers and problems too numerous to list, and will result in the human unit being permanently impounded. For free emergency service, call on JESUS.

DANGER: All human being units not responding to this recall action will have to be redeemed in the firey furnace of Truth and Love.

The SIN defect will not be permitted to enter Heaven so as to prevent contamination of that facility. Thank you for your attention!

— GOD

P.S. Please assist where possible by notifying others of this important notice of recall.

You may contact the *Father-Mother* at any time — 24/7 — by *'Knee-mail'* . . .

". . . because He Lives!"

High Flight

Oh! I have slipped the surely bonds of earth
   And danced the skies on laughter-silvered wings.

Sunward I've climbed,
   And joined the tumbling mirth Of sun-split clouds,
   And done a hundred things you have not
      dreamed of.

Wheeled and soared and swung high in the sunlit
   silence;

   And while — with silent lifting mind, —
   I've trod the high, untrespassed sanctity of
space —

   Put out my hand, — and touched the face of God.

John Gillespie Magee

"Forgive us our debts as we forgive our debtors."
  — *Jesus the Christ, at Matthew 6:12.*

Handling Presentments

ACCEPTANCE FOR VALUE
via the IRS

Write somewhere on the presentment (the bill) by hand the following (at an angle) so it will stand out.

> Accepted for Value
> Per HJR 192 of 1933
> Exempt from Levy
> $ (exact dollar amount) Date (mo/day/year)
> Deposit to US Treasury
> Charge to (strawman's name in all caps)
> SSN 123-45-6789
> By (your signature in blue ink) - Agent
> Exemption 123456789

Endorse the back as you would a check.

sign your name in blue ink
authorized representative

If there's a voucher, use it as a money order to credit the charge.

Write this information on the voucher anyplace it will fit:

1 - *This is a Money Order*
2 - *Pay to the US Treasury*
3 - *The Date* (mo/day/year)
4 - *$???.??* (dollar amount if there is a place for it).
5 - *$???.??* (write out dollar amount by hand).
6 - *By John Smith, EIN 123456789*
7 - *Authorized Representative*

<u>DO NOT USE A4V TO MAKE PURCHASES</u> !!!

GIVE YOURSELF CREDIT

1099A form
May be ordered at no cost from
http://tinyurl.com/2966by

Lender - *your name, address, city, state, ZIP, and tel.*
Lender's ID - *your SSN without dashes* (123456789)
Borrower's ID - *your SSN with dashes* (123-45-6789)
Borrower - *corporation bill you want to settle.*
Account number - *corporation account on bill.*

- box 1 - *date accepted.*
- box 2 - *amount credited*
- box 3 - *blank*
- box 4 - *amount credited*
- box 5 - *blank*
- box 6 - *mark "Secured Property"*

Processing may take 60-90 days.

Note: <u>Do Not Cut or Separate scannable 1099A Forms</u>.

Send with Acceptance to IRS at one of the following:

IRS - Stop 4440
P. O. Box 9036
Ogden, Utah 84201

    IRS - CID
    Box 192
    Covington, KY 41012

IRS - Treasury UCC Contract Trust
1500 Pennsylvania Avenue, NW
Washington, D.C. 20220

SEE SAMPLE BELOW

Accepted for Value
Per HJR 192 of 1933
Exempt from Levy
(???.?? dollars) Date (mo/day/year)
Depostit to US Treasury
Charge to (strawman's name in all caps)
SSN 123-45-6789
By (your signature in blue ink) - Agent
Exemption 123456789

This is a Money Order

Pay to US Treasury

mo/day/year

???.?? dollars

(write out amount of credit-dollars loaned)

*By (your signature in blue ink) - Agent
Exemption 123456789*

Your Signature in blue ink
Aurthorized Representative

Note:

Copy A of the official IRS form 1099A appears in red. So do **not** file Copy A downloaded from the IRS website.

The official printed version of IRS form 1099A is scannable, but the online version printed off of the IRS website is not.

A penalty of $50 per information return may be imposed for filing IRS forms that the IRS cannot scan.

To order official IRS forms go to http://tinyurl.com/2966by

Or call 1-800-TAX-FORM (1-800-829-3676).

ACCEPTANCE FOR VALUE
Return to Sender

ACCEPTANCE FOR VALUE
Return to Sender

Write or stamp at an angle on the top part of the statement so it will stand out:

For rollover accounts:

> **Accepted for value and consideration and returned for value**
> **Per HJR 192 of 1933**
> **Exemption #:** (FRB routing #) (Bond #)
> **Date:** ___(month/day/year)_____
> **By:** __(John Henry Doe), Agent____

For accounts you want to close:

> **Accepted for value and consideration and returned for settlement and closure**
> **Per HJR 192 of 1933**
> **Exemption #:** (FRB routing #) (Bond #)
> **Date:** ___(month/day/year)_____
> **By:** __(John Henry Doe), Agent____

On the coupon/voucher:

1. Write in the amount in the space provided.
2. Sign in blue on the lower right as you would a check.
3. Write your (FRB routing #) (Bond #) on the bottom left.

If your statement does not have a coupon:

1. Make a copy of the statement.
2. Accept it for Value
3. Write "Coupon" or "Voucher" at the top middle of the page.
4. Write your (FRB routing #) (Bond #) on the bottom left.
5. Only accept the front page.

Your Bond # is the red letter & 8 digit number on the back of your Social Security Card.

The FRB routing # is the number of the Federal Reserve Bank from the index below.

	FRB routing #
A - FRB OF BOSTON	0110-0001-5
B - FRB OF NEW YORK	0210-0120-8
C - FRB OF PHILADELPHIA	0310-0004-0
D - FRB OF CLEVELAND	0410-0001-4
E - FRB OF RICHMOND	0510-0003-3
F - FRB OF ATLANTA	0610-0014-6
G - FRB OF CHICAGO	0710-0030-1
H - FRB OF ST. LOUIS	0810-0004-5
I - FRB OF MINNEAPOLIS	0910-0008-0
J - FRB OF KANSAS CITY	1010-0004-8
K - FRB OF DALLAS	1110-0003-8
L - FRB OF SAN FRANCISCO	1210-0037-4

Make out a 1099A in the normal way and mail it with your acceptance to the sender, C/O CFO (Chief Financial Officer).

Accepted for value and consideration and returned for value (or for settlement)
Per HJR 192 of 1933
Exemption #: (FRB routing #) (Bond #)
Date: _____(month/day/year)_____
By: ___(John Henry Doe), Agent___

Money Order

Pay to the Order of Sender

(Month, Day, Year)

$???.??

(write out the exact amount)

(FRB routing #) (Bond #)　　　　　　　　　　By (John Henry Doe), Agent

GIVE YOURSELF CREDIT

NOTICE OF ACCEPTANCE FOR VALUE
Cover letter to Sender
(OPTIONAL)

STRAWMAN'S NAME
LOCATION
CITY, STATE, [ZIP]

Date --------

ATTN CFO
[CFO'S NAME]
[ADDRESS of Corp. Headquarters]

NOTICE OF ACCEPTANCE FOR VALUE

Dear [CFO'S NAME]

"I accept the attached charge for value and return it for value discharged per Public Policy Insurance Bond HJR 192 of 1933 and UCC 10-104 and 1-104 which is my congressionally stipulated Right."

The United States, Inc. created a Tacit Mortgage on my private property without my knowledge or consent and is using it as collateral for borrowing *loans of credit* and *money substitutes* from the non-federal Federal Reserve Bank.

Under the laws of equity and the US Constitution The United States, Inc. cannot take private property for public use and put it at risk as collateral for loans without just compensation and without providing a Remedy for the recovery of *accrued interest* lawfully due me for the risk of its use of my assets and wealth.

The provisions of this Remedy are found in Public Policy HJR 192 of 1933, a.k.a Public Law 73-10, which suspended the Gold Standard and exempted US Citizens from paying their debts since the means of paying debts was taken away from them in 1933 and replaced with money substitutes that discharge debts in lieu of payment.

Public Policy Insurance Bond HJR 192 of 1933 is a superior bond that provides a Remedy for victims of President Roosevelt's Fraud, Unlawful Conversion of their credit, and Treason, and for Congress' complicity in these crimes. This unlawful conversion of credit created the Exemption upon which this debt write-off and discharge is based because of the 1933 Bankruptcy of the Corporate United States which exempts Congress from charges of Treason against the United States and indemnifies me and other citizens for their loss.

Your Invoice is a negative charge to the debtor — my *ens legis* (*government created*) strawman — but a positive charge to me, a Secured Party Creditor of the Corporate United States.

Everything in Commerce, under the UCC, is reversed. A bill to your debtor (which is my strawman) is an offer of his credit to me, a Secured Party Creditor of the corporate United States.

I am accepting his credit and returning it to you as a *mutual offset credit exemption exchange* to settle your charge against his account.

My endorsement of your presentment converts it into a Money Order Promissory Note that discharges your charge against my strawman with my *mutual offset credit exemption exchange* per Public Policy Insurance Bond HJR 192 of 1933.

You presentment (bill) is a demand for payment in *"lawful money of account of the United States"* postponed to when such *"lawful money"* is restored to circulation.

When Uncle Sam prints a $20 dollar bill, that bill must be paid by the corporate United States *upon demand*.

Secured Party Creditors of the corporate United States can tender a *mutual offset credit exemption exchange* to fulfill his strawman's obligation to pay with his private personal credit.

By accepting substitute dollar bills in lieu of money we loan our private credit to Uncle Sam. Therefore we are to be paid back corresponding "dollar for dollar" portions of our private credit on demand.

Accrual income can be *immediately added* as an asset to an existing account because accrual income is accountable as soon as it is *tendered and received* instead of when collected.

When a Secured Party Creditor of the corporate United States purchases or subscribes to something that he needs his *mutual offset credit exemption exchange* will discharge his "obligation to pay" in lieu of Federal Reserve Notes for no real money exists with which he can pay.

The United States has a **priority obligation** to the Secured Party Creditors of the corporate United States and a **secondary obligation** to the non-federal Federal Reserve Bank for its obligation to compensate its secured party creditors for its use of Federal Reserve Notes instead of cash.

Commercial Redemption is a legal administrative Remedy provided by Congress on June 5, 1933 via HJR 192 to exempt Congress from charges of Treason (*it's their law not mine*).

The Collective Entity Rule makes a clear distinction between a *natural person* created by God and the *fictional person* created by the state.

The Collective Entity Rule was first articulated in *Hale v. Hale, 201 US 43, 26 S.Ct. 370, 50 L.Ed. 652.*

"The innocent individual who is harmed by an abuse of governmental authority is assured that he will be compensated for his injury." — Owen.

This is an *Administrative Contract Remedy*. It is not tendering payment.

There is no money to pay anything. Contracts are already in place in the background of the State. I am accepting your presentment and authorizing you to *set-off* and *discharge* the debt with said credit.

There is no evidence refuting the statements made in this NOTICE OF ACCEPTANCE FOR VALUE, and the undersigned believes that no such evidence exists.

If you wish to dispute this NOTICE OF INFORMATION, do not hesitate to timely reply in writing within the next two weeks.

In witness hereof, I certifying on penalties of perjury that all the statements made above are true, correct, and complete, and not intended to mislead.

Very truly,
John Henry Doe
Secured Party Creditor

Appendix

28
The Business Of Business

Americans today are living under the most diabolical slave system ever concocted in the world. We are potential prisoners right now, because we don't understand how the **business of business** works on our bodies and our minds.

Fewer than 1% of the people on planet earth fully understand how deep the rabbit hole goes. It is a shock and starting point to begin to understand the madness that is going on all around us, that we do not see.

Basically, the first order of law is called **natural law.** As children of God we are all under *natural law.* Something happened in the process that removed us from *natural law* and placed us under **artificial law.** And that process took place when we were born.

Your artificial mirror image corporate entity strawman was created at birth through the birth certificate on which your mother was listed as **"informant"** when she *gave you over to the state.* This is evidenced by your all capital letters NAME.

At this point the Certificate of Live Birth, upon which your Birth Certificate is based, was sent to Washington D.C. where a bond was attached. This bond is for a significant amount of money. Through Social Security you are entered into a **cestui que trust** by your Social Security Card.

On the back of your Social Security Card are 9 digits — **1 letter and 8 numbers in red** : — your exemption bond.

These 9 digits indicate your ***priority exemption prepaid account*** which is used by different corporations all over the world. It is presumed to be intellectual property that has been abandoned; i.e. ***abandoned property.***

It is deemed to be *abandoned property* because you haven't claimed it. You haven't claimed it because you didn't know that it existed, and that corporations are using your ***priority exemption number*** to access it.

This is how the whole system is set up.

There is the flesh and blood person and there is a mirror image strawman. What you do in commerce is *not predicated upon the flesh and blood you,* it is predicated on your mirror image strawman.

Look at your driver's license, your birth certificate, the checks in your check book, any commercial document. The printed name is not you, the flesh and blood man, it is an artificially created corporate entity know as the strawman. And until you take commercial control of the strawman that is attached to you, *that has your name in all capital letters,* the state has total control of it instead.

This is how they have been manipulating everybody as a people. This is not predicated on race. Everybody is being pillaged by this fraud, no matter what color you are.

Unfortunately, with the prison system as it is now, blacks have been set up to be a permanent underclass to be railroaded through the prison system so their bonds can be used on a regular basis.

Unbeknownst to many — The United States is not a country; **the United States is a corporation.**

We need to understand these concepts and see them as they really are. U.S., U.S.A., **United States, means a federal corporation.**

"It is clear that the United States is a corporation." (534 Federal Supplement 724).

"It is well stated that the United States, et al, is a corporation originally incorporated on February 21, 1871 under the name of District of Columbia." (16 Stat. 419 Chpt. 62).

The United States was reorganized in bankruptcy by the 14th Amendment on June 11, 1878.

The United States is in bankruptcy reorganization per House Joint Resolution 192 on June 5, 1933, per Senate Report 92549 and Executive Orders 6072, 6109, and 6246, as a de facto government that was originally the 10 square mile tract of land ceded by Maryland and Virginia, comprising Washington D.C.

Originally the United States consisted of the 10 square miles of Washington D.C., and through contracts it contracted with different states to expand that name to the rest of the states, plus the territories, forts, and arsenals.

The significance of this is that **as a corporation the United States has no more authority to implement its laws against "we-the-people" than does the McDonald's corporation** — except for one thing — **except for the contracts we signed as surety for our strawman with the creditor bankers and corporate United States.**

These contracts which bind us together with the bankers and the United States **are not contracts with us,** but are contracts between the bankers and the corporate United States with our artificial entity "person" strawman which *appears* to be us but is not, and is spelled with all capital letters.

The Key is to know that the strawman is formed as a

corporation in order to control us, they had to create an artificial corporate entity to extend their power over the flesh and blood man.

And when we discover these hidden adhesion contracts and how they bind us by not revealing their true nature we begin to realize how we end up in submission to these corporations.

Check **the MicroPrint signature line** (MP) on the checks in your check book, which when magnified reads: *authorized representative authorized representative authorized representative* all across the signature line, because you, the flesh and blood man, are the ***authorized representative*** for the strawman attached to you.

Contrary to what we have been taught in the government schools, the U.S. citizen is the strawman, which is part of the corporate fiction, and we need to understand how this came into creation.

June 11, 1878, is the real birth date of the corporate United States. But we are not under that venue. We had a Republic at that time and they slowly moved us into the Democracy, the corporate structure of the federal state.

It is important, when thinking about freedom, that we distinguish ourselves (the flesh and blood man), from the corporate fiction belonging to the state. In 1933 we were presented with what was then known as Roosevelt's New Deal. This is when the corporate fiction began.

The ground work had been already laid out in the 14th Amendment. We thought the 14th Amendment meant freedom for the slaves. Incorrect. That was the beginning of the creation of United States citizens and their enslavement. Prior to the 14th Amendment there was no such thing as a United States citizen. We were and still are Americans. A

United States citizen is a corporate fiction that only exists within the Matrix of corporate affairs.

In 1933 the whole American economy collapsed. That was when President Franklin Delano Roosevelt instituted his New Deal. It was sold to us as the resurrection of the country back from bankruptcy by his heroic saving of the day. But he sold the country into bankruptcy, instead.

The United States had gone bankrupt as a country at the beginning of the Civil War in 1859.

Individual bankruptcy exists for 7 years, but for a corporation bankruptcy exists for 10 x 7 years, or 70 years. So the plan had to be renewed in 1929. This was the whole point of Franklin Roosevelt and his New Deal, as soon as he got into power.

(1929 + 70 = 1999 = two years prior to 9/11)

The real deal of the New Deal was a raw deal for the American people.

This is when Roosevelt gave us the Maternity act which made it mandatory that everyone thereafter had to get a birth certificate when a child was born. They attached a bond on that birth certificate and sold that bond to the International bankers as collateral for the National Debt so that commerce could continue. The International bankers own everyone strawman that exists. *If you haven't separated yourself from your strawman then you are also property of the state, i.e. a ward of the state.* And they're moving to collect on their assets.

When they created the birth certificate, they removed lawful money from circulation.

The Constitution says that the only gold is lawful money, so by removing gold from circulation they became an illegal government in fact. They replaced gold with Federal Reserve Notes. And to protect themselves, in case the people woke up to see that we were using unconstitutional money, they devised the HJR 192 bond.

They made everyone bring in all their gold. All new citizens of the United States were given 30 days to bring in all their gold and exchange it for Federal Reserve Notes (FRNs) which are now not backed by any *thing* of substance at all. FRNs are money substitutes that we've been striving for, and killing ourselves for, that are nothing but worthless instruments of debt.

This artificial money has value only because it is accepted and received as value. This is why the powers-to-be are in a panic about Homeland Security, and all of their other different things, because as people wake up, they are beginning to realize that these FRNs, that we've all been using, are useless. **They are just instruments of debt.** They are not backed by any *thing* at all.

HJR 192 of 1933 was set up so that sovereign Americans would be able to discharge all of their debts, public and private, with their exemption.

Your exemption is evidenced by the numbers in red on the back of your Social Security Card. Unfortunately, it has taken us since 1933 to figure out how to access our exemption bond because we were never told that our exemption existed or how to use it to discharge our debts.

Major corporations have been tapping into and accessing our exemption because we have never claimed it and it is considered to be "abandoned" property.

HJR 192 of 1933 is an Insurance Remedy to "indemnify" (to reimburse) "we-the-people" for the loss suffered because of the government's treasonous acts of default.

Congress gave us ("we-the-people") HJR 192 of 1933

to discharge our debts, *but if we had never figured it out, that would have been our problem* — not the government's concern.

This is basically how they covered themselves when they introduced this fictitious form of money.

We've been taught in our **"Prussian school system"** how to navigate commerce. We're probably the least sophisticated of all Americans in understanding how they are navigating the **business of business** in the commercial world. We were never exposed to its rules and we were never meant to find out.

One of the key things that we must keep in mind is that **the United States Corporation is under bankruptcy reorganization, and under bankruptcy reorganization all the rules have been changed.**

It is actually **the reverse** of everything we've been taught in the government schools. And this is one of the reasons why we've experienced so much poverty and pain.

29
As It Is Today

From the United States Congressional Record, March 17, 1993 Vol. 33, page H-1303. Speaker-Rep. James Traficant, Jr. (Ohio) addressing the House:

"Mr. Speaker, we are here now in chapter 11. Members of Congress are official trustees presiding over the greatest reorganization of any Bankrupt entity in world history, the U.S. Government. We are setting forth hopefully, a blueprint for our future. There are some who say it is a coroner's report that will lead to our demise.

It is an established fact that the United States Federal Government has been dissolved by the Emergency Banking Act, March 9, 1933, 48 Stat. 1, Public Law 89-719; declared by President Roosevelt, being bankrupt and insolvent. H.J.R. 192, 73rd Congress, session June 5, 1933 - Joint Resolution To Suspend The Gold Standard and Abrogate The Gold Clause dissolved the Sovereign Authority of the United States and the official capacities of all United States Governmental Offices, Officers, and Departments and is further evidence that the United States Federal Government exists today in name only.

The receivers of the United States Bankruptcy are the International Bankers, via the United Nations, the World Bank and the International Monetary Fund."

These entities, *the International Bankers, the World Bank and the International Monetary Fund,* now control everyone's strawman, and are in the process of getting ready to cash in.

> *"All United States Offices, Officials, and Departments are now operating within a de facto status in name only under Emergency War Powers. With the Constitutional Republican form of Government now dissolved, the receivers of the Bankruptcy have adopted a new form of government for the United States. This new form of government is known as a Democracy, being an established Socialist/Communist order under a new governor for America. This act was instituted and established by transferring and/or placing the Office of the Secretary of Treasury to that of the Governor of the International Monetary Fund. Public Law 94-564, page 8, Section H.R. 13955 reads in part: "The U.S. Secretary of Treasury receives no compensation for representing the United States."'*

Basically they are telling you here that Timothy Geitner doesn't get paid by the American people. He works for the Federal Reserve and the International bankers who pay his salary. Actually, the office of Secretary of the Treasury about whom we have been taught, was dissolved in 1926.

What we have now is a trust located in Puerto Rico known as the U.S. Treasury. This is why Puerto Rico would never be separate and free. It is a Commonwealth where they discharge all debt and do all their scams in Puerto Rico because it is a tax to the United States and not in it. This is where most of the Treasury activity takes place. Also in the scam, they had to change the court system as well.

In *Thompkins v. Erie Railroad,* in 1938, the entire criminal justice system was changed from Public Law to Public Policy, which is in alignment with the corporations and corporate law. This is when we went under Admiralty. This is why no Bar Attorney in the United States can refer to any case prior to 1938. Such would serve as an automatic disbarment. In placing the court under Admiralty jurisdiction — we are all currently in an Admiralty court system, because in Admiralty you're operating under *color of law* and not law itself.

They did the ultimate flip flop in the court system, and this is why it is impossible to seek any kind of fairness or justice in the court system.

When you go to court, in the court system of today, you're looking at the flag with a gold fringe. This is letting you know that it is an Admiralty Maritime flag; it's the flag of the sea not the flag of the land. They moved the water line back and put everybody under Admiralty jurisdiction. This is why banks show an Admiralty flag to let you know you're in an Admiralty jurisdiction.

Under Admiralty jurisdiction you're operating under the law of the sea, and at no point would you know otherwise when going into the courtroom that you're operating under Maritime jurisdiction.

Most people are in debt, so they're just recycling the debt. You can owe GMAC, say, and GMAC sells the debt to an attorney for 10 cents on the dollar, and the attorney comes after you and harasses you. And they *may* even take you to court, and in court when anybody makes a claim against you they have to make out an affidavit for sworn testimony, and if you read the paper-work, they're saying right from the start, "It's alleged that so and so owes this much money."

All this can happen under color of law, that's presumed to be law, unless you have sense enough to challenge it and object. Everything that they're dealing with is colorable. We have a colorable jurisdiction, a colorable court, colorable claims, and, basically, you have to force the point and demand proof that this "alleged" debt even exists, because all these credit-card companies, every credit-card corporations, and even your employer is using your exemption.

And if you want to challenge them, when they send you a bill, ask them for a copy of their 1096 tax form, their 1099 OID, their INC and their PRC. These are all documents that prove that you are the principal, the creditor, the fiduciary creditor and principal, and that they are listed on all these documents as the fiduciary debtor. The are using your exemption because you don't know about it. And they are taxing you for it.

Because we are in a bankruptcy, all of these corporations are insolvent. The only real money out there (real credit) is you and me — that's it. They are insolvent. But because we are under Admiralty color-of-law jurisdiction, they get to flip-flop it and make it seem like *you are insolvent* instead of them. And they are actually using your exemption when you pay on these credit cards every month. So just by asking them to produce their 1096 tax form, their 1099 OID, their INC and their PRC, you will see that your name is listed as the principal, as the fiduciary, the creditor and the principal.

We are the creditors! They are using our exemption without which this whole system would crumble and collapse. And they are listed as the fiduciary debtors because they are insolvent. The exemption is worth millions of real dollars, and we've been studying this and researching this and we finally have dissected how to tap into our exemption by using an International Bill of Exchange under the guidelines of UNITRAL — the UN International Trade Law.

There's an International Promissory Note and International Bill of Exchange. You can use the IBOE on pre-existing debt and the IPN to buy things. This is how they've been tapping into our exemption.

There are several chapters throughout the Bible that talk about the worst thing you can possible do *is be a debtor,* and they have slapped all their debts upon us. The National Debt is probably about nine-trillions dollars and counting.

According to the US Code the National Debt should never exceed 6.5 trillions dollars. The day that the National Debt went over that limit was the day we experienced 9/11. All the banking records of the bonds were housed on the 1st floor of the World Trade Center. That's the real reason why the debt had to go.

We are at the point now where, when you're stopped by the police, they're putting into their computers all the updated latest Admiralty stuff. They're beginning *the assessment process.* They're putting your strawman into the computer and collecting through your exemption. It's listed as your CUSIP or AUTOTRIS number, and this is basically how they begin their paper trail. So when the case goes into the court system (when you're arrested), a bond is immediately placed on those charges for "x" amount of dollars.

There's really no such thing as criminal charges — all charges are civil. It's all about the money. Even murder.

Murder goes for 4 million dollars.

So you can discharge the criminal charges and "get-out-

Money Doesn't Grow On Trees

of-jail" free. And this would be done through a Money Order Bill of Exchange. But this is not a simple thing to accomplish. It can be done, but it's a very complex process. Once you go in talking AUTOTRIS/CUSIP, they're like, "Oh, he knows the entire scam."

And that's usually the end of the rope with the proper paper-work. You would begin with a Letter of Rogatory that would show that you are the foreigner, flesh-and-blood person, and that you're foreign to the corporate jurisdiction.

They always keep the sentencing separate from the trial. The sentencing is where they lock the charges, of the strawman, to the Federal Bureau of Prisons. After sentencing, they ask, "Do you accept?" "Do you understand the charge?" Most people, by and large, say "Yes."

"Do you accept 10 years?" She said "No." "Do you accept 5 years?" She said "No." "Case dismissed." She refused to be the surety for the Strawman.

This is all contract. When you sign your Driver's License, its the vilest contract that puts you into bondage because you don't understand that its an adhesion contract. Whenever you sign your name, starting today, just put "agent" after your signature. That way you are not liable for the Strawman. You are the *agent* for the strawman.

The only people obligated to pay an income tax are those people working for the federal government. If you are not a government employee you legally and lawfully do not have to pay taxes. And there would be a set of documents you would submit to support that.

Begin doing your own research. Being free is not free — is not easy. This is why they've created the Homeland Security, and why fighting in public can put you in jail under some code.

This is why they're criminalizing everything, so that they can have access to you.

With the National Debt, which is well over nine trillion dollars, the prison system is funding the whole works. And because they making stupid sums of money doing this they're now wanting to expand the system to the general public.

Even though you may not have personal debt, every United States "citizen" is responsible for about $30,000 dollars of this National Debt. This is why they're having the concentration camps, and why your hearing about the "useless eaters they are talking about. Everything is being prepared to move on everybody.

They're fixing up the streets so that tanks can come through. They're getting prepared to make even more money off the population because unbeknownst to the populace, they're responsible for the National Debt. So its critical that we begin to think sovereignly and begin to start to separate ourselves from the artificial corporate fiction strawman.

At the very least begin to sign as "agent."

30
After Moving In For $16 He's Ready To Share Info

WFAA Bio by CASEY NORTON, July 14, 2011, Updated Saturday, Jul 23.

FLOWER MOUND TEXAS — **A little-known Texas law and a foreclosure could have a man in Flower Mound living on Easy Street.**

Flower Mound's Waterford Drive is lined with well-manicured $300,000 homes. So, when a new neighbor moved in without the usual sale, mortgage-paying homeowners had a few questions.

"What paperwork is it and how is it legally binding if he doesn't legally own the house?" asked Leigh Lowrie, a neighboring resident. "He just squats there."

Lowrie and her husband said the house down the street was in foreclosure for more than a year and the owner walked away. Then, the mortgage company went out of business.

Apparently, that opened the door for someone to take advantage of the situation. But, **Kenneth Robinson** [not related to publisher: publisher is white] said he's no squatter. He said he moved in on June 17 after months of research about a Texas law called **"adverse possession."**

"This is not a normal process, but it is not a process that is not known," he said. "It's just not known to everybody."

He says an online form he printed out and filed at the Denton County courthouse for $16 gave him rights to the house. The paper says the house was abandoned and he's claiming ownership.

"I added some things here for my own protection," Robinson said.

The house is virtually empty, with just a few pieces of furniture. There is no running water or electricity.

But, Robinson said just by setting up camp in the living room, Texas law gives him exclusive negotiating rights with the original owner. If the owner wants him out, he would have to pay off his massive mortgage debt and the bank would have to file a complicated lawsuit.

Robinson believes because of the cost, neither is likely. The law says if he stays in the house, after three years he can ask the court for the title.

He told News 8 his goal is to eventually have the title of the home and be named the legal owner of the home.

"Absolutely," he said. **"I want to be owner of record. At this point,** because I possess it, **I am the owner."**

Robinson posted "no trespassing" signs after neighbors asked police to arrest him for breaking in.

Flower mound officers say they can't remove him from the property because home ownership is a civil matter, not criminal.

Lowrie and her neighbors continue to look for legal ways to get him out. They are talking to the mortgage company, real estate agents and attorneys. They're convinced he broke into the house to take possession, but Robinson told News 8 he found a key and he gained access legally.

"If he wants the house, buy the house like everyone else had to," Lowrie said. "Get the money, buy the house."

Robinson said he's not buying anything. As far as he's concerned, the $330,000 house is already his and he has the paperwork to prove it.

PUBLISHER'S COMMENTS

Right on! This guy filed an Affidavit of Adverse possession and now is staying in the house, legally. This ought to renew some interest in the **adverse possession** topic.

Most folks commenting about adverse possession don't understand it.

According to the law the person taking possession (a **"disseisor"**) has a claim of possession as soon as he moves in with intent to claim it as his own. His claim doesn't ripen into "perfect title" until the statutory period has elapsed (usually 7-10 years depending on the state), in this case apparently three years.

But he does have a claim of title, and the only person with a better claim is the mortgage company. That means the mortgage company is the only **"person"** who can legally kick him off the property now.

Hmm, so how do you defend against the mortgage company?

I think one should demand to see the **original promissory note**, since without it the lender has no standing to bring a lawsuit. And considering that most mortgages between 2002 and 2008 were sold to investors, the lenders probably no longer have that note.

But naturally the only reason the neighbors are so mad is that they are ignorant enough to pay for mortgages that they do not have to pay for. **If they looked into the retrieval of the original promissory note or the fact that no consideration was given for the mortgage thereby no le-**

Money Doesn't Grow On Trees

gally binding contract.

"Ignorance is bliss" is not always the rule. This case shows what a little know-ledge can do for you; and in this case score yourself a house for $16.

This will teach people that being a willfully ignorant slave in the system seldom pays.

Since he has possession he can file a Common Law Lien against it, and a Labor/Mechanics Lien, under Common Law.

These will put him in the position where he will be very tough to remove. Anybody coming against him will have to pay those liens before any title insurance will bind. Before the bank can do much, it has to undo all that and pay off the liens. These liens, if done right, are testimony to his **Affidavit of Adverse Possession.**

No equity judge can lawfully overturn testimony or alter such facts as recorded in commerce under common law.

This looks like a much better way to go than buying a home — unless you can A4V the debt away fast — even then this looks cheaper, **less down payment in FRN's.**

See video:
http://tinyurl.com/4xry4wl

31
Lawful Basis of Acceptance for Value

"No State shall make any THING but gold and silver Coin a Tender in Payment of Debts" — Article I, Section 10, Constitution of the United States of America.

The Europeans who came to North America were 'grub-staked' by others, probably the East India Trading Company and the Bank of England. It was a huge venture that required the investment of money to get it started. So the 'colonists' got their start based on hard money loans back in the days of hard money.

Once the colonists were established, they came together and incorporated in order to deal with the collective burden of the debt. The first incorporation was under the Articles of Confederation. The purpose of the Articles was two fold: first, to protect the interests of the creditors and secondly, to protect the assets of the colonists who were working to establish a new economy and a new country.

Later it was found that the Articles were weak in dealing with international contracts and the enforcement of Admiralty/ Maritime concerns. So the Articles were rolled into the Constitution for the united States of America which pulled together the loose ends left by the Articles.

Now since the people were trying to stave off bankruptcy liquidation and preserve the fruits of their labors, the Constitution operated in a bankruptcy reorganization mode. And since it was operating in bankruptcy, the law forum of the national government had to be Admiralty based on cargo hold insurance.

Bankruptcy reorganization exists in Admiralty law while *bankruptcy liquidation* exists in common law. Therefore, common law has always been offensive to the national government, while the states function on common law and liquidation. So there is this distinction between the bankruptcies operating in the national versus the state governments.

But later, when the national government was forced to stop using gold and silver for money, it ceased to mint it and even passed a law demanding that all **US citizens** turn in their gold, and once the gold was turned in they made it illegal for **US citizens** even to own gold.

This caused a dilemma in commerce. If there was no money, how would the people carry on commerce?

Well, as a *substitute* for money, the government went to the Law Merchant law forum for the solution and adopted notes and bills of exchange; or what has been called, negotiable instruments. Law Merchants had successfully used notes and bills for centuries with complete success, so their way of accounting in trade and commerce was adopted for use by the citizens of the United States

The US took up the use of bills of exchange and notes under the Negotiable Instruments Act of the 1800's. This later evolved into the Uniform Commercial Code which states the rules and regulations of commerce using notes and bills of exchange instead of silver and gold.

So with this new form of *money,* a new form of *accounting* had to be introduced, double entry bookkeeping; the balancing of credits and debits to reach equity, a zero balance. The zero balance in double entry bookkeeping has become a stumbling block for many who do not realize that this is the system of accounting under which we are operating today.

In other words, if it can be determined by double entry bookkeeping that equity and fairness exists... then everyone is satisfied and we go along our way. If the bookkeeping did show that there is inequity, then we must stop and *make adjustments* to restore fairness.

This change in *law forum* and *type of money* used in public commerce occurred around 1933 when the Federal Reserve Act passed in 1913 actually became law. Since it was not successfully objected to during the previous 20 year period, it became accepted in 1933, under the international law of proscription.

Our government was changed by the Federal Reserve Act and our commerce was revised. Commerce was changed from a *postpaid* debt system to a *prepaid* debt system.

It is true that a debt must be paid in order to have justice but this is not to say that the debt cannot be **pre-paid!** An anticipated debt can be **prepaid** before the debt is incurred or it can be **postpaid** after it is incurred.

Therefore, it was anticipated in 1933 — as a remedy for **citizens** regarding the public debt — that all public debt was declared by Public Policy to be prepaid.

The problem concerning this was that the government

never explained this to the citizens but kept it hidden from the people in a controlled environment.

So the people who depended on government regulation of their commerce, were kept from the knowledge of how this so-called *"New Deal"* really worked. So as a consequence, the people were robbed by those members of society who *did understand* how the system worked.

Once the government began to operate its fictions, then new considerations had to be launched.

The first steps that were taken had to do with sureties and bonds.

In Admiralty law everything works on insurance.

Insurance is a *future* indemnity (*compensation for loss*) against injury. In a perfect world of commerce we could function without insurance, but since we sometimes make mistakes, we must assure other people that we will not harm them with what we may do or are doing now.

This assurance (insurance) that we must provide could be in the form of an insurance policy or a bond.

A bond is a future indemnity against injury, and in addition to that bond we must provide a way to collect against that bond, or insurance policy, in the form of a surety (*a guarantee*).

So the people of the United States were enrolled into an association for the mutual benefit of each other where each member of the association cannot require any member of the group to pay *his fair share* of the association's debt. In other words, I will forgive the debts of other members as they forgive my debts, hence *consideration* is in the form of forgiveness of debt one to the other, as documented in "the Lord's Prayer".

This forgiveness of debt one to another is a benefit received which results in taxable events in that *fore-giveness* is not *giveness*. When we do something before it is required, it can only be a presumed event, so when we are "fore-giving" the remedy is created before the obligation to produce it.

So who provided the remedy before the time that it was required? And what do we owe that benefactor when we find out who bestowed the benefit? In theology we call it a *tithe;* in commerce we call it a *tax.*

In theology we pay tithes to the Creator in *substance.* In commerce we pay taxes to the Government in *bookkeeping entries.* In the earth we harvest substance, but in commerce we accumulate more paper debt.

So we pay in kind. We tithe to the Creator in substance; and we are taxed by the Government in more debt.

Returning back to the decade of the 30's we see how this "forgiveness of debt" system occurred.

It is important to understand the difference between a shadow and the **thing** that produces the shadow. We receive *light from a sun* many miles away (*that gives life to every* **thing** *on the earth*). We don't see the light until it strikes a **thing** which it cannot pass through.

For example: When light strikes our body, there it stops or is reflected in another direction. But if you look directly away from the sun, you will see the absence of light caused by your body, as a shadow. The shadow is the proof that there is some **thing** between the shadow and the source of light; the sun.

The shadow is proof that substance exists. Without the substance the shadow could not exist.

Money Doesn't Grow On Trees

Ever since the 30's we have been dealing with a *shadow,* or *de facto* government. We deal with the absence of light when we work with the shadow, *the fictional government.* This being the case, when we deal with the fiction we are not dealing with substance, but with the absence of substance. So when we introduce substance to the fiction problems arise.

In the *de facto* government, when the decision was made to go to double entry book-keeping and *money of account,* rather than *money of exchange,* a bond or surety had to be created to protect the creditors of the bankruptcy.

The bond that was created is an *umbrella bond* (or *supersedeas bond*) that is the *guarantee (or insurance policy; called public policy*) that a citizen does not have to pay a public debt with substance.

That *insurance policy (or guarantee*) is **HJR 192 of 1933** which is elsewhere codified in the UCC. **HJR 192 of 1933** is the indemnity bond that covers *compensation for loss* provided for any liability.

Since **HJR 192 of 1933** is the *guarantee* that a debt need not be paid in substance, **IT BECOMES THE PAYMENT IN FACT.**

Now what is the surety for that bond? What does the insurance policy insure? What is the *guarantee* backing **HJR 192 of 1933**? The surety cannot be found in the *shadow,* in the fiction. It is found in the *substance* that creates the shadow.

The surety is the people! The surety is the substance they produce by their labor! The *evidence* of this surety is the *birth certificate.*

The people are insuring themselves by pledging their

labor as a guarantee that their bookkeeping is correct! Since the people are the creditors, or the funders, of the substance that they produce by their energy, all substance publicly produced must be returned from the fiction to the creditors of the public domain who are the people.

So **HJR 192 of 1933** is the *prior agreement* of all the members of the venture called the association known as America, that we will abide by the Lord's Prayer!

When the disciples asked Jesus how to pray he told them, among other things, to ask the Lord to "forgive us our debts, as we forgive our debtors…" (Matt. 6:12). The debts in question were previously anticipated, and the remedy created before the debt.

Might this not be read instead, "forgive us our debts, via **HJR 192 of 1933**, as we pledge to forgive our debtors…", this way too. This is the same process, indeed.

Appreciation of wealth is a direct provision of God's grace.

Since the people insure their commercial activity in the public domain by accepting liability for the public debt, the people are the *creditors* of the bankruptcy. **The people are the *sponsors* of their credit.**

The United States has been operating in a Chapter 11 Bankruptcy reorganization in which the Filer of the bankruptcy is the **trustee and debtor in possession**, so if any creditor of the bankruptcy dishonors his pledge to support the bankruptcy with his credit, the trustee will liquidate the creditor to the amount of his dishonor because he has become delinquent.

The creditor had the obligation to settle the debt with his credit, with the debtor, but he refused to do so when asked.

Any request that the debtor makes to the creditor for more credit for the bankruptcy must be honored by acceptance. If not accepted, the creditor becomes a delinquent creditor in debt to the bankruptcy and gets liquidated by the **debtor in possession,** instead.

Whenever a debtor comes to the creditor and says, "forgive me my debts" and the creditor does not forgive the debtor by providing his credit, the Lord will call him to account for dishonoring the prepayment policy regarding debts.

In theology this is blasphemy of the Holy Spirit, but in commerce it is violating the public policy of the state. It is a dishonor of a benefit the creditor already received when he became a member of the association and guaranteed to its other members that he would forgive their debts.

Question: what public liabilities are we required to forgive? Answer: any liability shown on a double entry bookkeeping account.

If a certain matter cannot be ledgered in double entry accounting it is most likely a private matter to be resolved not in the public domain, but in the private realm instead.

A public request for adjustment will come directly to the all capital lettered name trust account; i.e., JOHN H. SMITH. This is an attempt to attach a debt onto the bond of the "JOHN H. SMITH TRUST". To do so is a violation of public policy by failing to forgive that debt.

Instead of settling the thing in the present, the attempt is made to enslave the creditor in some future event by attaching his bond. We prevent that by taking the "bill" that is sent to the "bond" and pulling it back into the present, by accepting the strawman debtor's request for credit and returning the credit to the original presenter of the bill for settlement and closure of the account.

When this is done we have defeated the scheme to enslave the creditor in some future event by his attachment of our bond.

Acceptance for Value insures the proper accounting in the double entry bookkeeping that needs to be done in order to adjust the account to zero.

SPECIAL FEATURE
HJR 192 of June 5, 1933

JOINT RESOLUTION TO SUSPEND THE GOLD STANDARD AND ABROGATE THE GOLD CLAUSE, JUNE 5, 1933

H.J. Res. 192, 73rd Cong., 1st Sess.

Joint resolution to assure uniform value to the coins and currencies of the United States.

Whereas the holding of or dealing in gold affect the public interest, and therefore subject to proper regulation and restriction; and

Whereas the existing emergency has disclosed that provisions of obligations which purport to give the obligee a right to require payment in gold or a particular kind of coin or currency of the United States, or in an amount of money of the United States measured thereby, obstruct the power of the Congress to regulate the value of money of the United States, and are inconsistent with the declared policy of the Congress to maintain at all times the equal power of every dollar, coined or issued by the United States, in the markets and in the payment of debts.

Now, therefore, be it

Resolved by the Senate and House of Representatives of the United States of America in Congress assembled, That

(a) every provision contained in or made with respect to any obligation which purports to give the obligee a right to require payment in gold or a particular kind of coin or currency, or in an amount in money of the United States measured thereby, is declared to be against public policy; and no such provision shall be contained in or made with respect to any obligation hereafter incurred.

Every obligation, heretofore or hereafter incurred, whether or not any such provisions is contained therein or made with respect thereto, **shall be discharged upon payment,** dollar for dollar, **in any such coin or currency which at the time of payment is legal tender** for public and private debts.

Any such provision contained in any law authorizing obligations to be issued by or under authority of the United States, is hereby repealed, but the repeal of any such provision shall not invalidate any other provision or authority contained in such law.

(b) As used in this resolution, the term "obligation" means an obligation (including every obligation of and to the United States, excepting currency) payable in money of the United States; and the term "coin or currency" means coin or currency of the United States, including Federal Reserve notes and circulating notes of Federal Reserve banks and national banking associations.

SEC. 2. The last sentence of paragraph (1) of subsection (b) of section 43 of the Act entitled " An Act to relieve the existing national economic emergency by increasing agricultural purchasing power, to raise revenue for extraordinary expenses incurred by reason of such emergency, to provide emergency relief with respect to agricultural indebtedness, to provide for the orderly liquidation of joint-stock land banks, and for other purposes", approved May 12, 1933, is amended to read as follows:

"All coins and currencies of the United States (including Federal Reserve notes and **circulating notes of** Federal Reserve banks and **national banking associations**) heretofore or hereafter coined or issued, **shall be legal tender** for all debts, for public and private, public charges, taxes, duties, and dues, except that gold coins, when below the standard weight and limit of tolerance provided by law for the single piece, shall be legal tender only at valuation in proportion to their actual weight."

Approved June 5, 1933, 4:30 p.m.

RE: Item tendered for Discharge of Debt.

    The instrument tendered to the bank and negotiated to the United States Treasury for settlement is an **"Obligation of THE UNITED STATES,"** under **Title 18USC Sect.8,** representing as the definition provides a **"certificate of indebtedness...drawn upon an authorized officer of the United States,"** (in this case the Secretary of the Treasury) **"issued under an Act of Congress"** (in this case **public law 73-10, HJR-192 of 1933** and **Title 31 USC 3123, and 31 USC 5103) and by treaty** (in this case **the UNITED NATIONS CONVENTION ON INTERNATIONAL BILLS OF EXCHANGE AND INTERNATIONAL PROMISSORY NOTES (UNCITRAL)** and the **Universal Postal Union headquartered in Bern, Switzerland).**

HJR- 192 further declares **"every provision...which purports to give the obligee a right to require payment in gold or a particular kind of coin or currency...is declared to be against Public Policy; and no such provision shall be...made with respect to any obligation hereafter incurred."**

Making way for discharge and recovery on US Corporate public debt due the Principals and Sureties of THE UNITED STATES providing as **"public policy"** for the discharge of **"every obligation", "including every obligation OF and TO THE UNITED STATES", "dollar for dollar",** allowing those backing the US financial reorganization to recover on it by **discharging** an obligation they owed **TO THE UNITED STATES** or its sub-corporate entities, **against that same amount of obligation OF THE UNITED STATES owed to them; thus providing the remedy for the discharge** and **orderly recovery** of equity interest on US Corporate public debt due the Sureties, Principals, and Holders of THE UNITED STATES, discharging **that** portion of the public debt **without expansion of credit, debt or obligation on THE UNITED STATES or these its prime-creditors** it was intended to satisfy equitable remedy to, **but** gaining for each bearer of such note, discharge of obligation equivalent in value 'dollar for dollar' to any and all **"lawful money of the United States"**.

Money Doesn't Grow On Trees

Final Word

In the interest accruing debt-money system we have in America today, debts are not paid but are simply transferred to someone else by commercial transactions, and the interest on that debt continues to accrue, payable to the non-federal, Federal Reserve Bank, hence the federal, National Debt continues to expand.

Any charge that is accepted for value per a *mutual off-set credit exemption exchange* is extinguished at once, therefore interest on *that debt* ceases to accrue and add to the federal, National Debt.

As charges of debt continue to be accepted for value, and extinguished in this way, instead of being merely discharged and passed on to someone else, the federal Nation Debt will gradually be reduced, charge by charge.

When acceptance for value is adopted by a *critical mass of Accepters,* the federal National Debt may eventually, and peacefully become extinct.

"Forgive us our debts, as we forgive our debtors." — *Matthew 6:12.*

OTHER PUBLICATIONS

NESARA: National *Economic Security and Reformation Act*
http://tinyurl.com/c8u42q6

History of Banking: *An Asian Perspective*
http://tinyurl.com/boeehjl

The People's Voice: *Former Arizona Sheriff Richard Mack*
http://tinyurl.com/d62fyg3

Asset Protection: *Pure Trust Organizations*
http://tinyurl.com/btrjfqp

The Matrix As It Is: *A Different Point Of View*
http://tinyurl.com/ckrbkge

From Debt To Prosperity: *'Social Credit' Defined*
http://tinyurl.com/d2tjmw3

Give Yourself Credit: *Money Doesn't Grow On Trees*
http://tinyurl.com/d7tphuv

My Home Is My Castle: *Beware Of The Dog*
http://tinyurl.com/bmzxc2n

Commercial Redemption: *The Hidden Truth*
http://tinyurl.com/d9etg7w

Hardcore Redemption-In-Law: *Commercial Freedom And Release*
http://tinyurl.com/cl65vrz

Oil Beneath Our Feet: *America's Energy Non-Crisis*
http://tinyurl.com/btlzqxf

Untold History Of America: *Let The Truth Be Told*
http://tinyurl.com/bu9kjjc

Debtocracy: *& Odious Debt Explained*
http://tinyurl.com/cooqzuz

New Beginning Study Course: *Connect The Dots And See*
http://tinyurl.com/cxpk42p

Monitions of a Mountain Man: *Manna, Money, & Me*
http://tinyurl.com/cusgcqs

Maine Street Miracle: *Saving Yourself And America*
http://tinyurl.com/d4yktlw

Reclaim Your Sovereignty: *Take Back Your Christian Name*
http://tinyurl.com/cf5taxh

Gun Carry In The USA: Your Right To Self-defence
http://tinyurl.com/cdn3y3y

Climategate Debunked: *Big Brother, Main Stream Media*
http://tinyurl.com/d6gy2xz

Epistle to the Americans I: *What you don't know about The Income Tax*
http://tinyurl.com/d99ujzm

Epistle to the Americans II: *What you don't know about American History*
http://tinyurl.com/cnyghyz

Epistle to the Americans III: *What you don't know about Money*
http://tinyurl.com/cp8nrh8

Money Doesn't Grow On Trees

Made in the USA
Middletown, DE
19 October 2023

40891642R00115